D1544383

Cracking the Gnostic Code

THE SOCIETY OF BIBLICAL LITERATURE
MONOGRAPH SERIES

E.F. Campbell, Editor
Jouette M. Bassler, Associate Editor

Number 46
CRACKING THE GNOSTIC CODE
The Powers in Gnosticism

by
Walter Wink

Walter Wink

CRACKING THE GNOSTIC CODE
The Powers in Gnosticism

Scholars Press
Atlanta, Georgia

CRACKING THE GNOSTIC CODE

by
Walter Wink

©1993
The Society of Biblical Literature

Library of Congress Cataloging in Publication Data
Wink, Walter.
    Cracking the Gnostic code: the powers in Gnosticism/Walter Wink.
      p. cm. — (Society of Biblical Literature monograph series; no. 46)
    Includes bibliographical references and indexes.
    ISBN 1-55540-859-1 (alk. paper). — ISBN 1-55540-860-5 (pbk.:
alk. paper)
    1. Gnosticism. 2. Powers (Christian theology)   I.Title.
II. Series.
BT1390.W55 1993
299'932—dc20
                                   93-10143
                                   CIP

Printed in the United States of America
on acid-free paper

CONTENTS

PREFACE

No one made more of the concept of "principalities and powers" than the Gnostics, and in the process they developed one of the most radical views of evil ever propounded. Within the framework of Gnostic mythology, the Powers clearly dominate attention. Yet we have lacked an interpretive framework for understanding what it was in actual experience they were identifying as Powers. Consequently, most readers of Gnostic lore simply dismiss the Powers as superstitious remnants of a bygone past.

It is my thesis that these Powers were very real indeed, and that they were in fact the spirituality of the massive institutions and forces that controlled the ancient world. In my trilogy, The Powers (*Naming the Powers*, 1984; *Unmasking the Powers*, 1986; and *Engaging the Powers*, 1992), I examine the principalities and powers in the Roman world as a conceptual category for identifying the social, political, psychic, and cosmological forces that determine earthly existence. By applying the results of that study to the Powers in Gnosticism, we can attempt to comprehend the real spiritual forces with which its mystics and metaphysicians were wrestling.

The Powers are so central to Gnostic thought that virtually the entire Gnostic corpus deals with them. No study of the Powers would be complete without an analysis of their role in Gnosticism. No study of Gnosticism would be complete without an examination of the role played by the Powers in the Gnostic systems.

I am, confessedly, no expert on Gnosticism. But then, experts on Gnosticism are not all that conversant with the principalities and powers.

It is my hope that what is lost by my ignorance of some of the finer points of Gnosticism is compensated for in part by my three decades of reflection about the Powers.[1]

I have not attempted to disguise my own convictions in this study, though I have tried to keep them from violating the data. As Heisenberg taught us, the viewer is a part of the field being viewed. We cannot know something as it is in itself, but only as that with which we are in dynamic interaction. There are no such things as objective facts, pure history, or disinterested historians. Nor is it possible to understand material like the Gnostic texts by themselves. Understanding is always a hermeneutical enterprise, that is, it is a quest for the meaning of texts. And that meaning cannot simply be read off the texts, but is the result of a conversation between two worlds, ours and theirs. We can only render texts meaningfully if we interpret them in terms intelligible to ourselves. This requires the use of analogies from our own experience. Consequently, understanding these Gnostics becomes also a way of understanding more about ourselves and our world today. Why else would we bother to read them?

Since the discovery of the Nag Hammadi documents, scholars have been preoccupied with translating and coordinating Gnostic texts. Rather than simplifying the interpretive task, Nag Hammadi has rendered it infinitely more complex. Consequently, there has been remarkably little hermeneutical effort expended on Gnosticism since the magisterial work of Hans Jonas and Carl Jung. This study attempts to throw a single span across that hermeneutical divide.

My concern in this book is not to repristinate Gnosticism, but to interpret its symbolically-couched insights. I am not seeking to provide either a defense of Gnosticism or a refutation of it, but to identify the socio-spiritual sources of the distress reflected in its worldview, and to disclose the radicality—and limitations—of its response.

Christians have been especially fearful of Gnosticism because in many respects it represents the shadow side of Christianity. "Gnostic" has been a thunderbolt that theologians could hurl at any suspect idea that remotely resembled Gnosticism, and thereby throttle discussion. It has been the heresy of convenience. Christians have all too often projected onto Gnostics their own longing to burst the bonds of orthodoxy and sexual mores and to be "free spirits" answerable to no

---

[1] Scholars are still a long way from adopting an agreed upon definition of what constitutes Gnosticism. I will let the study itself provide a cumulative impression of this distinct yet elusive phenomenon.

earthly power. Gnosticism thus posed the ultimate threat to a hierarchical, dogmatic, institutional religion that had become the spiritual bulwark of the political and social order, and the church reacted with every weapon at its disposal, including genocide (killing over a million Gnostic Cathari in Europe in the thirteenth century, to cite only the most extreme example).

Without attempting to champion the Gnostic position, can we at least appreciate the motives that gave it rise? Is it possible that we might learn something from these ancient masters of the soul? Are there still here for us today (to seize on one of their own images), "treasures in the mud"?

My deepest appreciation to Karen L. King and Ron Cameron for their helpful comments on the manuscript, and to Edward F. Campbell, Jr., senior editor of the Society for Biblical Literature Monograph Series, for making its publication both possible and actual.

Abbreviations

ANRW	*Aufstieg und Niedergang der römischen Welt*
FRLANT	Forschungen zur Religion und Literatur des Alten und Neuen Testaments
GR	*The Gnostic Religion*, by H. Jonas. 3d ed. Boston: Beacon Press, 1970
HTR	*Harvard Theological Review*
IFG	*Images of the Feminine in Gnosticism*. Ed. Karen L. King. Philadelphia: Fortress Press, 1988
JTS	*Journal of Theological Studies*, New Series
LCL	Loeb Classical Library
MacDermot	*Pistis Sophia*, tr. V. MacDermot, ed. C. Schmidt. NHS 9. Leiden: E. J. Brill, 1978
Mead	*Pistis Sophia*, tr. G. R. S. Mead. London: J.M. Watkins, (1921) 1963
NedTTs	*Nederlands Theologisch Tijdschrift*
NH	Denotes a text found at Nag Hammadi
NHL	*Nag Hammadi Library*, rev. ed. Ed. J. M. Robinson. San Francisco: Harper & Row, 1988
NHS	Nag Hammadi Studies

NT Apoc.	*New Testament Apocrypha*, 2 vols. Ed. Edgar Hennecke and Wilhelm Schneemelcher. Philadelphia: Westminster Press, 1965
OG	*Le Origini dello Gnosticismo*. Ed. Ugo Bianchi. Leiden: E. J. Brill, 1967
RG	*The Rediscovery of Gnosticism*, 2 vols. Ed. Bentley Layton. Leiden: E. J. Brill. Vol. 1: *The School of Valentinus*, 1980; Vol. 2: *Sethian Gnosticism*, 1981
RPT	Religionstheorie und Politische Theologie
SBLDS	Society of Biblical Literature Dissertation Series
SBLMS	Society of Biblical Literature Monograph Series
SCJ/ECJ	Studies in Christianity and Judaism/Etudes sur le christianisme et le judaïsme
SGHR	*Studies in Gnosticism and Hellenistic Religions. Festschrift for Gilles Quispel*. Ed. R. van den Broek and M. J. Vermasseren. Leiden: E. J. Brill, 1981
SOR	Studies in Oriental Religions
TU	Texte und Untersuchungen
Vig. Chr.	*Vigiliae Christianae*
WUNT	Wissenschaftliche Untersuchungen zum Neuen Testament
ZNW	*Zeitschrift für die Neutestamentliche Wissenschaft*

1

CRACKING THE GNOSTIC CODE

What could conceivably have driven some Gnostics to reject the body, sexuality, the very world itself, and to describe these material creations as slime, a prison, mud, an aborted foetus, a miscarriage, excrement? In a culture permeated by Greek and Roman sculpture and the Greek ideal of beauty, in a religious milieu increasingly familiar with the Jewish and Christian affirmations of the goodness of the Creator and the creation, what brought about this startling conversion into the opposite? What deep betrayal led to denunciations of this good flesh, the temple of the Holy Spirit, as "thy stinking body, thy garment of clay, the fetter, the bond" — as the Mandaean text *Ginza* 430 puts it? What experiences caused the Gnostics to repudiate, so far as they were able, virtually every political and religious institution of the ancient world, along with a good deal of that world's moral codes, values, authorities, and traditions?

We can no more give a socio-political "explanation" for the origins of Gnosticism than we can for the rise of Christianity. The search for historical "causes" is itself an inappropriate extension of mechanistic thought into open systems, where even the tiniest increment of freedom invalidates causal analysis. We can, however, point to predisposing factors that may have inclined some people toward Gnosticism—though we are at a loss to explain why others, faced with the same factors, chose to remain or to become Jewish, or pagan, or Christian.

With the collapse of the city-states and the dominance of the Roman Empire, decisions affecting the fate of whole peoples were now decreed in far-off Rome. An unwieldy and heedless bureaucracy straddled the Empire. For Rome's conquered subjects, politics ceased to exist. The best and the brightest could no longer contribute to the shaping of history.

Life was privatized. Consequently, rootless intellectuals in the Empire found themselves alienated and adrift, having lost all sense of at-home-ness in a world grown too large, too impersonal, and too impervious to reform. In reaction, they withdrew into intellectual enclaves, isolated from the culture at large, and developed a contempt for legitimate authority that issued in the creation of a closed symbolic universe which only elect people like themselves could enter.[1]

The newly atomized masses found themselves, according to Hans Jonas, in a situation in which the part was insignificant to the whole, and the whole alien to the parts. The law of empire under which they found themselves was ". . .an external dispensation of dominating, unapproachable force; and, for them, the same character was assumed by the law of the universe, cosmic destiny, of which the world state was the terrestrial executor."[2]

The blemish which they saw in nature lay not in its chaos, however, but in an excess of order: the feeling of being suffocated under a comprehensive system of oppressive cosmic fate. Following Jonas' lead, Kurt Rudolph describes Gnosticism as a protest of the dependent petty bourgeoisie against a sense of political powerlessness and ineffectiveness in the context of the Roman Empire.[3]

---

[1] Carl A. Raschke, *The Interruption of Eternity: Modern Gnosticism and the Origins of the New Religious Consciousness* (Chicago: Nelson-Hall, 1980) 43–44.

[2] Hans Jonas, "Gnosticism and Modern Nihilism," *Social Research* 19 (1952) 440.

[3] Kurt Rudolph, *Gnosis* (San Francisco: Harper and Row, 1983) 292–93; Hans Kippenberg, "Versuch einer soziologischen Verortung des antiken Gnostizismus," *Numen* 17 (1970) 21–32; Rudolph, "Das Problem einer Soziologie and 'sozialen Verortung' der Gnosis," *Kairos* 19/1 (1977) 35–44. Rudolph believes that the first Gnostics were Jewish wisdom *literati* who represented a politically powerless lay intellectualism demoralized and estranged under the Empire. Peter Munz criticized Kippenberg's article (and by implication Rudolph's) in "The Problem of 'Die Soziologische Verortung des Antiken Gnostizismus,'" *Numen* 19 (1972) 40–51. See also H. J. W. Drijvers, "The Origins of Gnosticism as a Religious and Historical Problem," *NedTTs* 22 (1968) 321–51.

Henry A. Green, *The Economic and Social Origins of Gnosticism* (Atlanta: Scholars Press, 1985), argues that Gnosticism arose in Egypt as a result of the demonopolization and privatization of the Egyptian economy. Upper class Jewish intellectuals, alienated from Judaism and locked out of Greek society, sought consolation in a religion that declared a pox on all their houses. He acknowledges that this is a "necessary, but not sufficient," explanation of the rise of Gnosticism, but he fails to show why Gnosticism would have such a powerful appeal elsewhere in the Empire, where the demonopolization and privatization of the economy had not taken place, and those who responded to the Gnostic message were not upper class

Others have attempted to account for the Gnostic abhorrence of the world by pointing to the political disillusionment of Jews following their catastrophic defeats in the uprisings of 66–70, 115–117, and 132–135.[4] Perhaps also, some Christians, perplexed by the delay of the Kingdom and buffeted by persecution, found themselves turning their backs on earthly hopes entirely. There can be no question that sociological factors contributed to the rise of Gnosticism, but they remain just that—factors. They are not "causes." Gibbon characterized the period of the Antonine emperors (138–180) as the happiest in all human history. Rostovtzeff in turn depicted the mid-third century in darkest terms as the "time of troubles," when brigands could no longer be contained and soldiers infested the roads, competing with common thieves in fleecing the populace.[5] Yet Gnosticism flourished in both periods. Likewise, intellectual elites in all ages tend to be petty bourgeois who complain tiresomely about their powerlessness. Catastrophes, military defeats, and exile litter history; religious hopes are routinely disconfirmed. But these events have seldom produced anything resembling Gnosticism elsewhere or in other periods.

All these factors undoubtedly worked to incline certain people toward Gnosticism. But causal explanations confuse two quite different questions, according to Peter Munz: the question, Why did certain people at a certain time in a certain place conceive and elaborate the new mythic images that configure Gnosticism? and the separate question, Why did others later find such myths plausible?[6] What requires explanation is why the particular circumstances around the turn of our era should suddenly have issued in a new and unprecedented religion, spanning a thousand years, whose appeal reached from Gaul and Spain in the West to the eastern borders of the Roman Empire and beyond, into Babylon, Persia, and even Turfan in Chinese Turkestan. Appeal to local

---

Jewish intellectuals. Nor does his thesis account for the appeal of Gnosticism in other ages and places, including our own.

[4] R. M. Grant, *Gnosticism and Early Christianity* (New York: Harper & Row, 1966) 27–38; E. M. Yamauchi, "Jewish Gnosticism" *SGHR* 490–91. Grant later repudiated his view, but political despair among Jews was probably a contributing factor predisposing some of them to Gnosticism.

[5] See Ramsay MacMullen, *Soldier and Civilian in the Later Roman Empire* (Cambridge: Harvard University Press, 1963) 88–89.

[6] Munz, "The Problem of 'Die soziologische Verortung'" 41. C. Scholten denies that we have sufficient hard data to say what the social setting of Gnosticism was ("Gibt es Quellen zur Sozialgeschichte der Valentinianer Roms?" *ZNW* 79 [1988] 244–61).

circumstances might account for the germ of the idea, but not its wild proliferation. A universal cause, on the other hand, founders on the fact that not everyone became a Gnostic, that it was, in fact, with the sole exception of Manichaeism, a fairly class-stratified and delimited movement.

No doubt many factors came to bear on the rise of Gnosticism. But these factors were not the cause, only the indispensable context and incubator for a new life that burst upon the world with its own unique genetic code. We still have not learned how to speak about the emergence of the new in history. However close its parents, however tight the circle of its aunts and uncles and extended family, what came to birth in Gnosticism was unparalleled.

We are almost totally lacking in sociological data about the Gnostics. What we do have, however, in every Gnostic source known to us, is a prodigious preoccupation with the Powers. What Gnostics, Christians and pagans (and all the shades of gray between them) shared in that period was a common awareness of spiritual forces that were impinging on them through the massive institutions that had supplanted the world of the city-state and the ethnic kingdoms. They could not yet in most cases identify the institutional sources of their distress, but they were able to isolate these forces, as it were, by projection, and to fight them "in the air" as a way of winning some measure of freedom from their power. What they called principalities, powers, authorities, dominions, thrones, forces, angels, archangels, elements, and so forth were, on my hypothesis, the real experiences of the spirituality of the monolithic political, economic and social forces that dominated and often tyrannized their daily lives. As Pheme Perkins puts it, "The archons [rulers] in most Gnostic stories—especially the Chief Archon—behave very much as people saw the 'great ones' of the world behaving every day."[7]

Christians saw it as their task to engage these Powers in spiritual warfare aimed at delegitimating them at their spiritual root; that was what martyrdom for refusing idolatry was all about. Gnostics also sought to expose the illusory system spun by these powers in order that people might withdraw from their sway and escape them into the world beyond. Both agreed, however, that the world was in the grip of malignant, anti-human forces.

My hypothesis, developed at length in my trilogy on The Powers, is that all power has an inner and an outer aspect. The outer is comprised

---

7 P. Perkins, *The Gnostic Dialogue* (New York: Paulist Press, 1980) 171.

of the physical or visible elements, the inner by an invisible "interiority" or spirituality. In the first century these dual aspects of power were visualized mythically as "the heavens and the earth." Everything heavenly had its earthly counterpart, and everything earthly its heavenly. Nothing happened on earth without a simultaneous happening in heaven.

During the rise of materialistic thought that characterized the eighteenth century European Enlightenment, the heavenly was denied existence. Only that which can be felt, tasted, smelled, heard and seen, or reasoned about logically, was counted real. Today there has arisen a new appreciation for the reality of the spiritual. But we can scarcely go back to a two-storied universe; people today simply cannot imagine heaven as literally in the sky, or believe, with no less a thinker than Plutarch, that the moon was the repository of souls.[8] What we can do, however, is to reconceive the heavenly as the "within" or interiority of earthly reality:

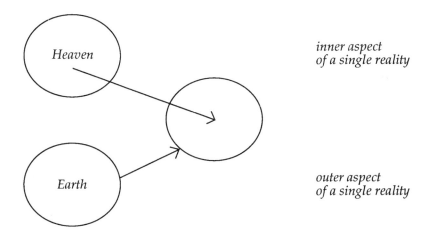

inner aspect
of a single reality

outer aspect
of a single reality

This hypothesis is indispensable for cracking the Gnostic code. For the Gnostics' protest against existence in the world is veiled. They appear to speak only of heavenly beings. But their language masks a vehement protest against the actual order of the world, in its socio-political as well as its spiritual aspects.

---

[8] Plutarch, *On the Face of the Moon* 943–44. Plutarch puts this belief in the mouth of the Stranger, to be sure, but probably agreed. Iamblichus, for his part, followed Heraclitus in thinking that souls descended from the Milky Way; others said from the celestial spheres (John Dillon, "The Descent of the Soul," *RG* 1. 358–59). Most modern people are simply no longer able to think that way.

The Roman Empire, for example, had its outer manifestations: the incumbent Caesar, his appointees, the governmental bureaucracy, palaces, temples, armies, tribunals, judges, the capital city, conquered territories, and so forth. But these outer forms of power had an inner, invisible, but equally palpable reality, symbolized by the worship of Roma and the Imperial Genius, the Roman gods, and the tributary gods subjected and harnessed to the Empire by the establishment of their temples in Rome. These represented the actual spirituality of Rome, the secret of its power to unite so many disparate peoples into a single political entity. These gods provided the empire's legitimation, morale, and the illusion of its eternity.

Some Christians, seeing with far different eyes, perceived the spirituality of Rome as Satan incarnate (Rev 12–13). Jewish writers also identified the Angel of Rome with Sammael and Satan and the Angel of Death.[9] Zosimos, a Gnostic writer, associated the chief Roman god Jupiter with Fate, and thus equated the spiritual center of the Roman pantheon with the contemptible jailer of this repressive world.[10] All three assertions were counter-discernments, minority reports on a spirituality which the vast majority of Rome's subjects either celebrated or accepted with stoic docility. Only three religions—Judaism, Christianity, and Gnosticism (the latter two in many respects children of the former)—attacked the idolatry of the Empire and its suffocating controls. The Jews actually fought, repeatedly. The Christians resisted, nonviolently. The Gnostics withdrew, invisibly.[11]

Whatever its political limitations, *Gnosticism provided a stunning revelation of the actual spirituality of the Roman world.* The Powers featured in Gnosticism—the Demiurge (Creator) and his Archons ("rulers")—were, to some degree at least, the symbolic distillate of the negative

---

[9] I. P. Culianu goes so far as to argue that the Demiurge concept evolved from the notion of an angel-prince (*archon*) who as chief of the heavenly council received the title "Prince of the world" and was occasionally mistaken as God or the creator. Since this was also the title due the angel of Rome, because it ruled the world, and since Rome's angel Sammael had already been identified with Satan and with the angel of Death, it was a short step to regarding the "Prince" or Chief Archon of this world as the *evil* Creator of the world ("The Angels of the Nations and the Origins of Gnostic Dualism," *SGHR* 78–91). For Gnosticism, see *NH Hyp. Arch.* 94:25–26.

[10] The pagan Gnostic alchemist Zosimos, *Omega* 3–4, p. 229 lines 16ff.; in Jonas, *GR* 96.

[11] The Cynics and other related philosophical movements also provided sharp criticism of the institutions of the Empire, but they were highly individualistic and did not constitute an organized opposition.

experiences of Roman rule. As Hans Kippenberg puts it, "In other words, aggression against the Greeks and Romans is displaced and transferred to the Archons. Accordingly, mythological events come to reflect political events."[12]

The seeds planted in Jewish apocalyptic and wisdom literature that had come to bud in the New Testament teaching on the Powers now bloomed to full flower in Gnosticism. The unique contribution of Gnosticism to world religions was the capacity of the Gnostic visionaries to discern the oppressive spirituality of the current world order. But they were able to perceive this felt reality only by projecting it out onto the screen of the cosmos and mythologizing it as a narrative about the spirit's entrapment by and redemption from the Powers. This myth was in turn spun out as metaphysical teaching, but it was fundamentally grounded in experience.

Carl Jung called the Gnostics the first psychologists. This is not quite true. They were metaphysicians who projected the psyche into their metaphysics, but it was not psychology until Jung identified and withdrew the projections by means of interpretation.[13] But their flights of introspection also succeeded in apprehending (still in a projected mode) *the inner shape of outer things*: the spirituality of institutions, of priesthoods, of moral constraints and legal demands, of the Roman Empire itself, and most pervasively of all, the spiritual atmosphere of domination that had incarnated itself in one empire after another since the rise of conquest states. At times the myths they wove became too cerebral, and lost their relationship to the primary intuitions percolating up from the imaginal realm. Their great new discovery, however, was the insight that, to a limited but startling degree, the psyche itself is the product of extraneous powers and forces alien to the true self. The fundamental religious impulse of Gnosticism was fury that the very soul itself had been invaded and taken captive by the Powers.

Jung's psychology, so valuable for understanding Gnostic texts, has often been misinterpreted by his followers along subjectivistic, individualistic, privatized lines. On the contrary, the self in Jung's psychology is ultimately a *social* category; it represents the transcendence of the ego's Demiurge-like delusion that it alone exists as the highest power. We need to learn to see the self not only as the totality of the person, but also as the network of relationships in which a person exists. Individuation

---

[12] Kippenberg, "Versuch einer soziologischen Verortung" 220–21.

[13] John A. Sanford, in a personal communication. Sanford thinks Jesus was the first depth psychologist (*The Kingdom Within* [Philadelphia: J. B. Lippincott, 1970]).

properly means being able to transcend mere ego concerns and the insistent demands of the personal psyche, and to embrace all that is.

Jung suggested that ". . .the idea of angels, archangels, the 'principalities and powers' in St. Paul, the archons of the Gnostics, the heavenly hierarchy of Dionysius the Areopagite," all come from "the perception of the relative autonomy of the archetypes." These archetypes are collective, a "legacy of ancestral life;"[14] but they were also, we now need to add, the actual spirituality of the current social and political order. Hence they were not ancestral only but also a new configuration of objective external forces which were being transmitted to the antennae, as it were, of the visionary Gnostics. What was introjected from the social world was in turn projected out onto the cosmos. The "withinness" of socio-political reality was thus brought to consciousness the only way it could have been in that time: by being displayed on the screen of the universe.

As Paul Ricoeur puts it, "To manifest the 'sacred' *on* the 'cosmos' and to manifest it *in* the 'psyche' are the same thing. . . Cosmos and Psyche are the two poles of the same 'expressivity'; I express myself in expressing the world; I explore my own sacrality in deciphering that of the world."[15]

Dreams provide a helpful analogy. Once people regarded the images of dreams as premonitions of outer events; now they are understood as, more likely, representations of a person's own inner struggle for individuation. Similarly, the Gnostics apparently regarded their visions as objective data about the heavenly realm; today we can interpret them as, among other things, a source for divining and unmasking the inner spirituality of an entire social order and its imprinting on the psyche. All they

---

[14] Carl Jung, *Two Essays on Analytical Psychology*, 2nd ed., Collected Works 7, Bollingen Series 20 (Princeton: Princeton University, 1966) 66, 77. See also *Aion*, Collected Works 9.2 (1959) 222: "Gnosis is undoubtedly a psychological knowledge whose contents derive from the unconscious. It reached its insights by concentrating on the 'subjective factor,' which consists empirically in the demonstrable influence that the collective unconscious exerts on the conscious mind. This would explain the astonishing parallelism between Gnostic symbolism and the findings of the psychology of the unconscious." Again, in *The Symbolic Life*, Collected Works 18 (1980) 652–53, Jung suggests that the Gnostics derived their knowledge of the higher realms from the unconscious. "This discovery results not only in the possibility but also in the necessity of supplementing the historical method of explanation by one that is based on a scientific psychology." Historical explanations alone are futile, because they can only reduce Gnostic ideas to their less developed forestages but cannot understand their actual significance.

[15] Paul Ricoeur, *The Symbolism of Evil* (New York: Harper & Row, 1967) 12–13.

lacked was the hermeneutical key provided by a social reading of depth psychology, in order for their remarkably perceptive protests to have become actual resistance, and for their accurate mythic impressions to have been translated into analytic categories.

More than one Gnostic text reflects the nature of this process. The goal of *gnosis* ("knowledge" or, better, "insight"), according to the *NH Gospel of Truth*, is to "know interiorly," to become "sons of interior knowledge,"[16] that is, to sink so deeply into the unconscious that one passes through the vestibule of merely personal contents and into the deep interior, where the psyche opens out to infinity, and is capable of receiving impressions from the whole collective experience of the race. Having penetrated to the interior, one discovers oneself, paradoxically, on the outside, dealing with the structures and forces of social and physical reality.[17]

Thus in *Pistis Sophia*[18] we read, "And all the angels and their archangels and all the powers of the height all sang praises to *the innermost of the inner*,[19] so that the whole world heard their voices. . . .." This interior singing nevertheless is heard by the whole world; radical interiority is social. At least one authentic means of entry to the collective is through the self.

So another text can say that the benevolent heavenly Powers, by looking into their own faces, perceived ". . .*gnosis* in relation to themselves. And their journey to themselves was their turning inward once again. . . .. And the hearing of their ears was the perception which is in their hearts."[20] Now when Gnostics speak of the fall and suffering of the spirits, they speak of themselves, notes Kippenberg; when they speak of the Demiurge (Creator), they are talking about the socio-political system that confronts them as alien.[21] What is projected onto the heavens is precisely the Gnostic vision quest: the audacious belief that by turning within, through radical introspection, one can uncover *the truth of the*

---

[16] *NH Gos. Truth* 32:23, 38–39.

[17] See my *Naming the Powers* (Philadelphia: Fortress Press, 1984) 143–45.

[18] *Pistis Sophia* I.3 (MacDermot, p. 6), emphasis added.

[19] Mead, 5, reads, "the interiors of the interiors."

[20] *The Untitled Text* 11, in *The Books of Jeu and the Untitled Text in the Bruce Codex* (ed. C. Schmidt, tr. and comm. by V. MacDermot; Leiden: E. J. Brill, 1978) 257. So also *NH Thom. Cont.* 138:15–18: ". . .you have (in fact) already come to know, and you will be called 'the one who knows himself.' For he who has not known himself has known nothing, but he who has known himself has at the same time already achieved knowledge about the depth of the all."

[21] Kippenberg, "Versuch einer sociologischen Verortung" 230.

whole cosmos. With the same passion that animates modern physicists in their search for the ultimate particle as the building block and clue to the universe, generations of Gnostics turned inward in a passionate search for the ultimate mystery of the cosmos, convinced, with an intuitive certainty beyond all reasoning, that the secret of reality lay, like a priceless pearl, in the cave of the unconscious, guarded by dragons.

How aware were they of what they were doing? Jonas doubts they were at all. He finds no evidence that the Gnostics understood the ascent of the soul as a schema for an inner evolution of the soul in this life, capable of being experienced in a progressive sequence of psychic states. Their reflections usually seem to remain at the level of myth, that is, as an objective account of an external event expected for the soul after its separation from the body in death.[22]

But there are a few notable exceptions. The *NH Treatise on the Resurrection* treats resurrection as a present experience, not simply as a future afterlife in heaven. *NH Thunder: Perfect Mind* states revealingly, "What is inside of you is what is outside of you, and the one who fashions you on the outside is the one who shaped the inside of you. And what you see outside of you, you see inside of you" (20:18–24).[23] And Jung himself could have authored Norea's retort to the Archons (rulers) who had raped her mother, Eve: "You did not know my mother; instead it was your female counterpart that you knew," that is, their own inner femininity.[24] So at least some writers in that period already perceived that the mythical drama was indeed a mystical path, and that the outer images depicted inner realities that could be disclosed no other way. But there is little evidence that they were able to expand this insight to include the spirituality of social institutions.

As long as a psychic content remains in the projected state, it is inaccessible for conscious reflection. Later monastic and Jewish merkavah mystics were to make an epochal shift; around the year 500 they began to speak of spiritual *descent* rather than ascent. Heaven was to be found, not

---

[22] Jonas, "Delimitation of the Gnostic Phenomenon—Typology and History," *OG* 107.

[23] *NH Thund.*, though found among Gnostic writings, is extremely hard to classify. This, however, does not affect its value as a witness to conscious awareness of the mechanism of projection. Raymund Schwager finds an even earlier indication that the process we call projection was recognized as such in Wis 17:2–20 (*Must There Be Scapegoats?* [San Francisco: Harper & Row, 1987] 108–109). Plutarch may also have understood the phenomenon; see his *Dialogue on Love* (*Eroticus*), in *Moralia* (LCL 9; Cambridge: Harvard University, 1969) 352–55.

[24] *NH Hyp. Arch.* 92:23–25; so also *NH Orig. World* 117:12–14.

in the sky, but in and through the soul.[25] But the step to withdrawing the cosmic projections and reconceiving them as elements in inner spiritual development could not have been made by the later mystics apart from the spiritual topographical maps these earlier Gnostic explorers of the soul had made, having blazed a trail into the Unknown by the only means available, then or now. The Gnostics helped prepare the way for this step toward inner awareness, even if they were unable to take it fully themselves.

Jonas notes that the word "projection" is the literal equivalent of the Greek *probole*, which is "the constant term used [in the Church Father's reports on Gnostic teaching] for that creative activity more commonly translated as 'emanating.'"[26] Several texts actually speak of the birth of the gods as a process of "projection," perhaps reflecting the very internal process the Gnostic visionaries were themselves undergoing. Thus the *NH A Valentinian Exposition* speaks of the Son as "the projector of the All and the very hypostasis of the Father" (24:22–24). Later the same author relates how "Pronoia [Forethought or Providence] caused the correction to project shadows and images of those who exist from the first and those who are and those who shall be" (36:10–15). And again, "After Jesus brought them forth he brought forth. . .the angels. For simultaneously. . .her consort projected the angels, since he abides by the will of the Father" (36:21–28, 1st ed.). This text is very instructive, for it equates "projecting" and "bringing forth," an expression used repeatedly in this literature.[27] That is, the entire creative process of the universe is regarded as one in which Mind (Nous) autocreates by "conceiving" and "throwing forward" (*pro-jacere*) onto the surface of the universe the visionary realities discovered by an inner process of spiritual discernment.

---

[25] G. G. Scholem, *Major Trends in Jewish Mysticism* (New York: Schocken Books, 1965) 46–47. See also Jonas, *GR* 165–66, and "Myth and Mysticism: A Study of Objectification and Interiorization in Religious Thought," *Philosophical Essays* (Englewood Cliffs, NJ: Prentice-Hall, 1974) 291–304.

[26] Jonas, *GR* 180 n. 8. Jonas summarizes the opening sentences of Valentinian Gnosis thus: "This Abyss took thought to project out of himself the beginning of all things, and he sank this project [sic] like a seed into the womb of the Silence that was with him, and she conceived." Similarly, the rest of the divine Powers are projected into being.

[27] See also the frequent references to the divine as *autogenes*, "self-creating" or "self-producing" (Index to *NHL*, 1st ed.—28 times). Simonian Gnosis speaks of the Nous (mind) "educing himself from himself and making manifest to himself his own thought" (Hippolytus, *Refutation of All Heresies*. VI.13; Jonas' translation, *GR* 105–106).

It is not adequate to assert, however, that ". . .one can and should regard the story of the primordial, inner-divine drama. . .as a kind of projection from human psychology."[28] This understanding of projection is reductionistic. The reality is more complex. As Robert Avens puts it, "The psyche is the projector and the projected in one."[29] The Gnostics knew too much about the autonomy and power of the archetypes to believe that God is merely a projection of human beings. According to Gilles Quispel, they rather expressed in their imaginative thinking that the world and humanity are a projection of God. And this, says Quispel, is correct.[30] Individuation *is* the work of the divine within the self. As a contemporary Gnostic, Charles Upton, commented in a letter to me, when we withdraw projections (in the Jungian sense), we begin to see that we have not created the world, but that the ego (the false creator or Demiurge) is an emanation from, and totally contingent upon, God, the true Creator.

No doubt the process is really reciprocal. We might say then that the God-human relationship is, at one level, an endless series of progressively modified reimagings, in which we and God mutually project and are projected upon under the impetus of continually new experiences.[31]

My thesis, in short, is that the heavenly visions, heavenly journeys, and revelations of the divine order beyond this phenomenal world so rife in that period were not simply symbolic depictions of the process of

---

[28] Jonas, "Delimitation of the Gnostic Phenomenon" 107.

[29] Robert Avens, *The New Gnosis* (Dallas: Spring Publications, 1984) 23.

[30] Gilles Quispel, "Gnosis and Psychology," in *RG* 1. 31. "In the newly discovered writings of Nag Hammadi, it is said again and again that the world and man are projections." Barbelo looks down on the primeval waters which mirror her shadowy image, and "the world originates from [her] projecting activity" (p. 29).

[31] Charles Upton's comment to me on this paragraph is perceptive. Mutuality, he says, should not be portrayed so as to imply equality. God "needs" us for His/Her manifestation; we need God for our very existence, which is nothing other than God's manifestation, i.e., nothing in itself apart from God. God's "imaging" of us creates us, and is a conscious exploration by God of the implications of the Divine nature in the realm of dimensionality and manifestation (as opposed to God's direct knowledge of His/Her own essence, which knowledge *is* God). Our imaging God, on the other hand, is essentially idolatry: A veiling of the Divine Reality through all our attempts to understand It in terms other than Its Own. If God accepts this idolatry as true worship, this is by mercy alone, since God understands that we cannot begin to apprehend the truth except through imaginal veils—veils of manifestation which are eternally projected and eternally annihilated. And human consciousness, Upton concludes, is itself the greatest manifestation, the greatest veil.

personal individuation, as Jung has so brilliantly demonstrated.[32] They are also very precise chartings of the seismic upheavals shaking and shattering human existence in the era of Roman hegemony, and they register a total aversion to the whole world over which the Powers of that era held sway.

This thesis avoids the reductionism of certain sociological or psychological approaches, in that it regards the spiritual beings of Gnostic mythology not as a mystification of the material forces at work in the institutions and systems of that day, but as *the actual spirituality of those material forces and systems*. The demonic spirits, whose hegemony over that world these Gnostics discerned, were real. But they were not disembodied phantoms flapping in the sky. They were the interiority or withinness—the essence, ethos, corporate personality, driving spirit—of the institutions and social arrangements that were the source of the Gnostic protest.

---

[32] In several essays, Jung did explore the impact of current political tendencies on the psyches of his patients; in a few he attempted to address contemporary events. See especially the essays collected in *Civilization in Transition*, Collected Works 10 (1964).

2

THE GNOSTIC MYTH

It is probably impossible to isolate a "core" myth of Gnosticism, so wildly did it mutate. Essential to most versions, however, is a story of how this corrupt world came to be. In some versions, evil is intrinsic to reality; destructive powers existed from all eternity. This approach characterizes the more Eastern forms of Gnosticism such as Mandaeism and Manichaeism. The more typically Western versions, such as Valentinianism, tended to regard evil as an inner-divine process, devolution, and tragedy. It is the latter view that the Nag Hammadi discoveries most illuminate, and since these texts have not till recently been available (as the Eastern texts have been), I have chosen to focus on the Western and, most especially, Valentinian, forms of the myth. The *NH Tripartite Tractate* will serve as our guide, though I have drawn on other Gnostic sources as well.[1] Since it is not our objective to survey all Gnostic positions, but only to comprehend the dynamic at work in their understanding of the Powers, it is sufficient for our purposes to illustrate that usage from those texts that have left us clues, which can then be employed to understand other texts in which that dynamic is assumed without being made explicit. Aided by our theory of the Powers, it may now be possible to interpret the Gnostic treatment of the Powers in a manner that honors both the generative impulse and lasting contribution of Gnosticism.

---

[1] E. Thomassen comments, "The singularly rationalistic approach of the author [of the *NH Tri. Trac.*] makes the metaphysical structure of his system transparent in such a way that the tractate may serve as an introduction to Gnostic thought in general as well as illuminate Valentinian theology and mythology in particular" ("The Structure of the Transcendent World in the Tripartite Tractate [NHC I,5]," *Vig. Chr.* 34 [1980] 358–75).

In the beginning, then, there was only an ineffable and unknowable divine being or source, wholly good. Among the multitude of heavenly beings that it "brought forth" from itself, one, sometimes a male god, more often a female god (Sophia), errs and creates an inferior reality, which in turn autocreates in increasingly disfigured forms, arriving finally at matter.[2] For many Gnostics, Creation was not followed by a Fall, as in Judaism and Christianity; Creation *was* the Fall. They were a single, tragic event.

Central to this devolution into matter in many texts is a Demiurge, or Creator god, often equated with the God of the Hebrew Scriptures, who is ignorant of all other powers above him, even his Mother, Sophia.[3] Humanity is created by this Demiurge, but thanks to the intervention of higher powers, a divine spark is implanted within the prison of human flesh. Salvation consists in a person's being awakened from sleep, or sobered up from spiritual drunkenness, recognizing the hideous lie that is the world, and being liberated from the control of the Demiurge (also called Archon or Logos) and his Powers. In what may be a later, literalizing version, at death the redeemed spirit sloughs off the body of flesh, slips past the seven planetary rulers (Archons) by means of secret passwords, and receives a "spiritual body" in the high heavens beyond, where the self becomes one again with the God beyond the gods.

The fundamental mythic insight here is that human beings are socialized into an alienating and alienated world that is antithetical to the emergence of true selfhood and, in fact, is positively hostile to it. The world-atmosphere is dominated by a "counterfeit spirit" that seduces the soul and leads it astray, drawing it to works of wickedness and handing it over ". . .to the authorities who came into being through the archon

---

[2] In the Iranian stream of Gnosticism, the cosmic flaw is not due to an inner-divine development, but rather to a basic dualism in the divine itself. Even in the earlier Western versions, Sophia was not viewed as the aeon whose independent action brought about the tragedy that constitutes human existence. It is later writers who tend to lay the blame on her (Deirdre J. Good, *Reconstructing the Tradition of Sophia in Gnostic Literature* [SBLMS 32; Atlanta: Scholars Press, 1987]).

[3] The Demiurge does not appear in all Gnostic traditions, especially the less Jewish or Christian, more Hellenistic ones. And in the earliest systems which do feature a Demiurge, he is not a parody of the biblical Creator. A few texts depict him as in strife with Satan (or describe Satan as his rebellious son or father), or see him as capable of repentance and restoration, or even portray him as instrumental in humanity's salvation (Ugo Bianchi, "Le problème des origines du Gnosticisme," *OG* 17–20; Jarl E. Fossum, *The Name of God and the Angel of the Lord* [WUNT 36; Tübingen: J. C. B. Mohr, 1985] 7–8; M. J. Edwards, "Gnostics and Valentinians in the Church Fathers," *JTS* 40 [1989] 40.

[Demiurge], and they bind it with chains and cast it into prison."[4] The prophets of Israel and the early Christians had criticized the political and religious order and authorities, but in Gnosticism there was for the first time a categorical rejection of all extraneous rule and authority. Not only all institutions, but matter, the body, sex, the world itself, were a cosmic blunder that fragmented the deity. The religious impulse is thus not only to save oneself from this irrational and lugubrious mistake, but to rescue the Godhead as well, bringing the soul-sparks scattered in the prison of matter back to the divine and restoring it at last to its primordial unity.

The world will then be dissolved; nothing else will be saved. The Powers—the social structures of reality, political systems, human institutions such as the family or religion—all will be brought to an end. These Powers will not be "restored" to their proper roles in service to humanity, since they have no proper role in Gnostic thought. They will be utterly exterminated. Perhaps, as one source avers, the Powers are, unknown to themselves, used by the high God for good; perhaps they can be made to serve the ordering of society in the interim before they are destroyed.[5] But there is no dialectic of good and evil within the Powers. Despite significant exceptions, the tendency is totally to demonize them.[6]

What made Gnosticism distinctive as a religious orientation was the belief in two levels in the supraterrestrial world, each with its own God, one in or above the highest heaven (the Ogdoad, or eighth heaven), wholly good; the other, in the lower heaven (the Hebdomad, or seven heavens), evil or at best confused, ignorant, arrogant, or limited.[7] According to the *NH Tri. Trac.*, the material world-system (*oikonomia*[8]) is the result of the "arrogance" of the Logos, who created an entire order of delusionary powers: "likenesses, copies, shadows, and phantasms, lacking reason and the light," by which to stupify and coerce humanity

---

[4] *NH Ap. John* 26:20–27:11.

[5] *NH Tri. Trac.* 89:28–90:1.

[6] Jonas commented early on (1966) that the Gnostic mood had ". . .an element of rebellion and protest about it. Its rejection of the world, far from the serenity or resignation of other nonworldly creeds, is of peculiar, sometimes vituperative violence, and we generally note a tendency to extremism, to excess in fantasy and feeling." ("The Gnostic Syndrome: Typology of its Thought, Imagination, and Mood," *Philosophical Essays* 272.)

[7] Simone Pétrement, *A Separate God* (HarperSanFrancisco, 1990) 10.

[8] *NH Tri. Trac.* 77:3; by contrast, *sustasis* is used for the system of the Pleroma, or highest heaven (Harold W. Attridge and Elaine Pagels, "The Tripartite Tractate," *Nag Hammadi Codex I* [(2 vols.; ed. Attridge; NHS 22–23; Leiden: E. J. Brill, 1985] 2. 306).

(78:32–35). There follows a remarkable analysis of the Domination System:

> They [the Powers] thought of themselves, that they are beings existing by themselves and are without a source, since they do not see anything else existing before them. Therefore they live in disobedience and acts of rebellion, without having humbled themselves before the one because of whom they came into being.
>
> They wanted to command one another, outrivaling one another in their vain ambition. . ... They were brought to a lust for power over one another according to the glory of the name of which each is a shadow, each one imagining that it is superior to the others.[9]

One could scarcely conceive of a more accurate description of the chaos of Powers each vying for ascendancy at the expense of the others. Together they create an invisible yet palpable world atmosphere that legitimates the quest for domination by institutions and empires. In Jonas' words, the Gnostics divested the ancient system of rule of its sanctity; they ". . .degraded. . .the alleged dignity of an inspired 'hierarchical' order to a naked display of power. . .which at the most could exact obedience but not respect."[10]

These Powers in turn gave birth to "hylics"—human beings entirely lacking the divine spark, "as fighters, as warriors, as troublemakers, as apostates in disobedience, as lovers of power" (80:5–10). Seeing what he had created, the Logos "was at a loss and astonished" (80:14). One has the clear sense here of a programming error running out of control. It was now impossible ". . .for him to make them cease from loving disturbance, nor was it possible for him to destroy it [the world]" (80:20–22). The Logos (regarded here, paradoxically, as a principle of irrational rationality, of coercive order) repented of the bedlam he had created, but the delusional power system was now firmly in place, and he could not destroy it. This abortive attempt to create a world in imitation of the higher, divine order is "an illusion of similarity," an "imitation of the system which was a unity" (82:19–20; 81:4–5, 1st ed.).

---

9 *NH Tri. Trac.* 79:12–32, 1st ed. See also the Sethian-Ophites: "The first of them, Ialdabaoth [the Demiurge] despised the Mother in that without her permission he made sons and grandsons—angels, archangels, excellences, powers, and dominions. When they had been made, his sons turned to a struggle against him for the primacy" (Irenaeus, *Against Heresy* V.30.5; tr. R. M. Grant, *Gnosticism: An Anthology* [London: Collins, 1961] 51).

10 Jonas, *Gnosis und spätantiker Geist* (FRLANT 33; Göttingen: Vandenhoeck und Ruprecht, 1934) 1. 214–15.

Human beings, that is to say, are able to create systems that appear harmonious, appear to imitate the divine order and hence seem deserving of worship or at least obedience; but in fact they are only sustained at the cost of unbearable injustice and violence. Those in the grip of such systems, even those most brazenly exploited by them, exist as though in ". . .forgetfulness and heavy sleep; being like those who dream troubled dreams, to whom sleep comes while they—those who dream—are oppressed" (82:26–31). These are somewhat like what Marx called the "lumpen proletariat," who acquiesce willingly in their own exploitation, except that these hylics are to be found in every class.

The Powers next fashioned the "psychics," people with the divine spark but so deeply mired in matter and desire that their salvation is problematic at best. "They were submerged in acts of violence and cruelty, as is normal in cases of mutual assault, since they have a lust for power and all other things of this sort. . .while none of them remembers the exalted one nor acknowledges" the true God on high (84:11–24, 1st ed.). In some Gnostic systems these psychics cannot be saved, in others they can, by rigorous asceticism and faithful obedience to the precepts of true religion. But only a third category of people, the "pneumatics," the truly spiritual, are free from the Powers and capable, even now, of escape to the Pleroma or true heavens.[11]

This threefold division of humanity is devastating when applied to individuals, especially within a given community, and the Christian churches stoutly resisted such distinctions. Who knows, after all, who is capable of turning to God? Such categories usurp the prerogatives of God, who alone knows the human heart, and prompt arrogance in those who believe themselves saved regardless of their subsequent behavior.

Nevertheless, this threefold distinction does have a certain utility; Paul himself is moving in this direction in 1 Cor 2:12–3:4. Some people do seem to have irretrievably sold themselves to the lust for domination (hylics), others can be helped to see domination for what it is and to abandon it (psychics), while still others never seem to have been tempted by domination from the start (pneumatics). And the tractate reminds us that the issue is finally theological, not characterological: everything rests on the capacity to acknowledge the Exalted One (84:22–24). The lust for power is itself a compensatory mechanism to mask the vacuity of a God-empty heart.

---

[11]   E. Pagels, "Conflicting Versions of Valentinian Eschatology: Irenaeus' Treatise vs. *The Excerpts from Theodotus*," *HTR* 67 (1974) 35–53. Pétrement sees the threefold anthropology discussed here as far more complex (*A Separate God* 181–210).

Behind the pessimistic elitism of this anthropology lies a profound recognition of humanity's capacity to be socially conditioned to forget its own most precious essence. And that is as true and problematic today as when these documents were first written. "Knowledge of the truth which existed before ignorance. . .is liberation from the servile nature in which all those suffered who originated from an inferior thought."[12] Beneath the obfuscating metaphysical drama in which it is couched, this statement points to the undeniable fact that most people *are* molded by an "inferior thought" and implanted with a "servile nature." The vast majority of people do suffer from a negative self-image. Their minds are filled by the media with "inferior thoughts." They learn to accept, without blinking, suicidal political and environmental policies. Gnostic criticism would be hard to translate into democracy, with the latter's odd faith in the common people, but it certainly identifies one of the factors that makes democratic governance such hard work.

On the other hand, the Gnostics might have had a real appreciation for democratic checks and balances on the exercise of power. In the very imperfect world over which the Logos rules, the angelic Powers are set against each other, using their lust for power to keep each other in check. Each watches over the race or nation or administration which has been entrusted to it. "There are kings, there are lords and those who give commands, some for administering punishment, others for administering justice, still others for giving rest and healing, others for teaching, others for guarding" (100:12–18).[13]

Those who think they can escape "this world" by playing one Power off against another discover that their attempts to save themselves lead simply to further entanglement. Life within the psycho-physical world of the Archons is one vast labyrinth. One cannot gain exit from the Domination System by means of powers embedded in that system. Unredeemed life is thus experienced as a series of flights from one Power by means of another Power from which one must subsequently be freed as well. "Having once strayed into the labyrinth of evils, the wretched [Soul] finds no way out."[14]

---

[12] *NH Tri. Trac.* 117:28–38, Rudolph's translation, *Gnosis* 268.

[13] Like the writers of the New Testament, the Gnostics move without warning from descriptions of spiritual forces to statements about human agents. This is consistent with the understanding of the Powers as at once the outer and inner manifestations of a single socio-spiritual phenomenon (see my *Naming the Powers*, parts 1 and 3).

[14] Naassene Psalm, in Hippolytus, *Refutation* V.10.2, translated by Jonas, *GR* 52.

One theme these unwitting social critics returned to over and over is the arrogance of power. According to the Valentinian Gnostic Ptolemy, for example, Sophia "projected what she had learned from the Saviour" and created the Demiurge (Creator), who "formed all that came after himself, being secretly moved by his mother." Hence "the Demiurge believed that he had created all this of himself"—that is, that it was all his own projection. But in fact he had made them because Sophia had prompted him to do so. "He made the heaven without knowing the heaven; he formed man without knowing him; he brought the earth to light without knowing it. And in every case, they say, he was ignorant of the ideas of the things he made and even of his own mother, and imagined that he alone was all things."[15]

To modern ears there is something strangely familiar about this way of thinking. Sophia "projects" the Demiurge, who in turn believes that all she has prompted him to create are his own projection. Is this not the irony of the Western intellect shaped by the Enlightenment: Promethean humanity, persuaded that it alone bears the light of consciousness in a mute and darkling universe, creates the gods? This has been the titanic revolt of modernism: that the spiritual world is a mere "projection" of the Demiurge, here identified with the human ego.

These texts assert otherwise: Sophia created the Demiurge, and moved him to create. This is a crucial corrective of the arrogance of the Renaissance. The higher powers project the lower, not the lower powers the higher. We do not "think up" archetypes; they force themselves on us willy-nilly from a region of unawareness totally beyond our ken. The archetypes give rise to thought. Thought can in turn modify the archetypes, if it stays in close touch with the ongoing experience of the unconscious. But when thought becomes autonomous ("arrogance"), it drifts off into cold abstractions devoid of all power to enhance life. Such an alienated reason was the basis of Blake's figure Urizen ("your reason"), the epitome of a reason depraved through the exclusion of all else but reason.

Even when we do project inner experience onto the screen of the cosmos, as the Gnostics did, it bears repeating that we project out what was first projected in. We do not create the gods; they are there already. They are not invented but revealed. We shape the gods in our own image, to be sure, but if we are in actual contact with the divine and not

---

[15] Irenaeus, *Against Heresy* I.5.1–3; Werner Foerster's translation, *Gnosis* (Oxford: Clarendon Press, 1972) 1. 135–37. See also *NH Hyp. Arch.* 86:27–31 and B. Layton's commentary, "The Hypostasis of the Archons (Conclusion)," *HTR* 69 (1976) 31–101.

just engaged in god-talk, the divine shapes us as well, and first: our very minds can reflect on these things because they are created in the image of God.

Put differently, at the personal level the Demiurge represents the alienated ego, while at the level of the collective unconscious it represents the whole alienating world in its forgetfulness of the Source of life. The Demiurge is thus the spirituality of a world where human beings live estranged from the true wellsprings of life, and imagine themselves as little demiurges who are the sole creators and gods of this world. The alienated personal ego of "this world" is thus the socialized product of the Domination System, just as the alienating spirituality of the Domination System is the product of millions of alienated egos trapped in an illusory fantasy. The Demiurge is thus at once the unredeemed personal ego and the world-atmosphere of hybris that plays itself out in the wars and conflicts born of collectivities of ego-centered people placing their own mistaken views of their short-term interests above the best long-term interests of themselves and the whole.

The Demiurge "made the heaven without knowing the heaven;" the spirituality behind the socio-political world is ignorant of its actual Source. The Domination System has a spirituality but does not know that it does. It behaves in a "heavenly" mode as the "within" of material things, but without knowing the source of its own withinness. Corporations, families, nations, the media, all trade in "atmospherics," image making, ideological warfare: "the air will be diseased" (*NH Asklepius* 73:18). They foster patriotism, feelings of solidarity, morale, corporate cultures, with no recognition that they are handling spiritual things, or of the One in and through and for whom they exist.

Let me give a contemporary example. In her Masters thesis, "Physician-Nurse-Patient Relationships: A Nursing Perspective,"[16] Hazel Schattschneider employs an understanding of the Powers to analyze the role of nurses in Canadian hospitals. She describes the hierarchical, patriarchal role of doctors, who are often cast, and sometimes cast themselves, as gods at the center of a cultus. They jealously guard their turf; hospitals are frequently run, not for the convenience of patients, but of doctors or administrators. Nurses, by contrast, are like the mother in a Victorian home, who does most of the managing and whose husband (the doctor) comes home periodically to check on the family and leaves

---

[16] Hazel Schattschneider, "Physician-Nurse-Patient Relationships: A Nursing Perspective," Master's Thesis, St. Stephen's Theological College, Edmonton, Alberta, 1988.

orders for the mother to carry out. Nurses are to be loyal to the physician, hide his mistakes, not question his orders, and protect his "aura of omnipotence" and institutional authority.

This milieu, which many nurses are trying to change toward a more collegial, interactive, relational set of power arrangements, is typically experienced as a system of "power over" rather than power sharing. If the doctor is "god," the nurse is an "angel," meek and calm, a handmaiden of docility in white. This imbalance in power, which exists despite common knowledge that nurses are central to the healing process and are healers in their own right, has created an unhealthy corporate spirit or "angel" in hospitals that desperately requires transformation. Nurses are routinely treated by doctors as inferiors; patients are often excluded from involvement in their own healing and even decisions affecting their very lives. Schattschneider calls for a liberation ethic that will change hospital hierarchicalism into mutual power sharing.

Critical to her argument is the assertion that it is not the personnel as such that create the problem (arrogant doctors, timid nurses, desperate patients projecting on both of them unrealistic hopes and fears), but the spirituality of the system that binds people into typified roles and responses. "For we are not contending against flesh and blood, but against the principalities, against the powers, against the world rulers of this present darkness" (Eph 6:12).

A medical doctor, reviewing her thesis, made a fascinating comment which she shared with me:

> I have difficulty in accepting, or even seeing the relevance of, [the idea of] demonic powers in the health care system. I accept that there is an outer and inner manifestation of power. Actually, I don't think that concept. . .is new, in any sense. It stands to reason that any organization will have both structure and policy, both forms and philosophy, both inner and outer—but "demonic"? . . .I also agree that "when an institution places greater value on its structure and tradition than on the dignity and worth of human being it has become demonic" (p. 39)—but I don't see where it applies.

The fact is that the concept of an outer and an inner aspect to all organizations, while self-evident once it is seen, is of very recent vintage. But what the doctor will not concede is that it has any relevance. He had never before in his life recognized that the system over which he helps preside has an "angel," and now, having been apprised of its existence, *denies that nurses actually experience the patriarchal power system of the hospital as dehumanizing, demeaning, and demonic,* even after reading an entire thesis full of examples.

In a similar way business professors now are beginning to talk about corporate cultures and symbolic systems, but do so in the usual reductionist, materialist mode. "Of course" businesses have a felt gestalt, an aura, an esprit de corps; but this insight does not cause people to recognize the pathology in the system or to engage in struggles for its transformation.

Charles Upton wrote me about a conversation held with a woman from a consulting firm that sets up drug treatment programs within large businesses.

> She approached us to say that, under new federal legislation which makes it easier for some companies to enforce drug testing, there was now a wonderful opportunity to force more and more workers into treatment programs, and that her firm's long-term track-record for successful treatment was over 70 percent. She also quoted statistics to the effect that one quarter of U.S. workers have drug or alcohol problems. While admitting that drug testing may sometimes be necessary, especially in environmentally sensitive industries (remember that the captain of the Exxon Valdes may have been drunk when the Alaska oil spill occurred), we also lamented the need for drug testing as a terrible and dehumanizing situation. This was totally beyond her comprehension. She went on to define large corporations as both "cultures" and "families," and to assert that the psychological problems of U.S. workers were a product of the biological family itself; according to her, large corporations were now in a position to heal these psychic wounds through forced treatment. We countered by saying that corporations are not families; that to view your boss as a parent is an example of unhealthy transference; that corporations are far too limited in the aspects of our humanity which they address to be classed as viable cultures; and that at least some of the blame for chemical dependency must be laid at the feet of corporations themselves, and the dehumanized conditions under which they sometimes force us to work. She reacted with incomprehension and defensiveness. That the corporate structure itself could be responsible in part for the addictions of its workers was to her a subversive and heretical concept: she was owned, or *possessed*, by the Archon of the Corporate World.

Like the Demiurge, those who run our institutions are tempted to believe that they have created all this themselves, and imagine that they alone are all things.[17] The Gnostic analysis of the power-complex of the Demiurge, far from being antiquated, renders a remarkably accurate

---

[17]   Valentinians, in Irenaeus, *Against Heresy,* I.5.3.

depiction of the spiritual effects of corporations and institutions that make their own welfare the highest good. In the past few centuries, the delusion of the Demiurge has descended to engulf the mind of Western culture as a whole: "He [the Demiurge], too weak to know anything spiritual, imagined that he was himself the only God and said through the prophets, 'I am God, and apart from me there is none else' (Isa 45:5)."[18]

Unfortunately, from my viewpoint, the Gnostics did not pass from this astonishing insight to an engagement with the Powers that might have attempted to recall them to their divine vocation. Indeed, the Gnostics have been, with some justice, pilloried for their social irrelevance. But we must be clearer than we have in the past that their escapism was born, not of bourgeois satisfaction, but an analysis so extreme and uncompromising that it left no room for social action or efforts at amelioration whatever. Curiously enough, extreme views of evil, which can tolerate no ambiguity or mix of evil in people and the world, generally end by being politically reactionary. Consider Thomas Hobbes' *Leviathan*, for example: human society is a war of all against the others; human nature cannot be improved. Hence a strong prince with centralized powers and an unfettered capacity to coerce is necessary in order to restrain the natural anarchy of people.

Hobbes was at least interested in politics. The Gnostics, despite the lucidity of their mythologically-depicted discernment of the political and social ills of their day, were never able to translate it into overt resistance. If evil is so utterly entrenched, endemic, and ineradicable, then there is nothing that can be done to fix or improve the present order. Thus the Gnostics were quiescent, waiting for escape to the other world, while the masters of greed escalated their war on life, unresisted.

---

[18] Ibid, I.5.4.

3

THE DELUSIONAL SYSTEM OF THE POWERS

Marcion, not himself a full-fledged Gnostic, accurately perceived that the God of the Old Testament was not consistent in all respects with the loving God revealed by Jesus, and propounded the view that the Jewish God was merely the Creator (Demiurge). Marcion's solution was appealingly simple—another flight from ambiguity—and the church resisted his thought tenaciously. But it is important to recognize the force of Marcion's ethical passion. He was the first to perceive with unstinting candor the degree to which *the God-image becomes captive to the Domination System and its needs for legitimation*. This notion was already latent in John 8:44, where the Fourth Evangelist asserts that the real father of the religious authorities is not the God whom they believe they worship, but Satan himself, that is, the spirit of the Domination System. The *NH Gospel of Philip* develops the same idea more diplomatically: "The rulers (archons) wanted to deceive humanity;" they took ". . .the name of those that are good and gave it to those that are not good, so that through the names they might deceive him [humanity] and bind them to those that are not good" (54:18–25). No one, however, has expressed this insight with the force of William Blake's judgment on Christendom: "Man must & will have Some Religion; if he has not the Religion of Jesus, he will have the Religion of Satan, & will erect the Synagogue of Satan, calling the Prince of this world, God; and destroying all who do not worship Satan under the Name of God."[1]

---

[1] William Blake, "Jerusalem," plate 52, in *The Complete Writings of William Blake* (rev. ed.; ed. David V. Erdman; Berkeley: University of California, 1982) 201.

We can watch this very process of "changing the names" happening to the Christian church, as it moved from persecuted sect to established religion. Language of the Powers had been common to all wings of the church, orthodox and Gnostic-tending alike, until Constantine began to coopt Christianity in 312. Soon the church became the official religion of the Empire, and its success became indistinguishable from the success of the Empire. In a radical reversal, preservation of the Empire became the decisive criterion for Christian ethical behavior.[2] The church moved from a position in opposition to the dominant society to being its chief spiritual support. Christians who had been earmarked as food for lions by Roman magistrates suddenly found themselves these magistrates' confessors. Much good came of this—the end of child exposure, gladiatorial contests, slavery, officially condoned moral dissoluteness—but the church paid with the loss of a fundamental social critique. It had brilliantly attacked the Domination System incarnate in Rome at the point of idolatry. When the christianizing Empire denounced idolatry, the church thought it had won. But the Domination System was still in place, and passed even more insidiously into the church itself, which found itself unable to resist using political power to suppress its rivals.

Not surprisingly, talk about principalities and powers now became an embarrassment to the emergent "Great Church." With the crushing of Gnosticism by the power of the "Christian" state, the category of the Powers was lost as a means of ethical discernment. The Powers were reduced to disembodied demons in the air, deprived of all institutional reference. Apologists for ecclesiastical ascendancy like Eusebius could not tolerate criticism of the imperium. It was not just heresy but outright sedition when Gnostics spoke like this: "Do you think these rulers have any power over you? None of them can prevail against the root of truth. . .these Authorities will be restrained."[3] And the fact that the Gnostics had made the Powers so central to their systems further brought the Powers into discredit at a time when the church was busy making itself one of the leading Powers.

It was only a matter of time then until the social theory of the atonement, so powerfully depicted in the Christus Victor imagery of Col 2:15,

---

[2] J. Denny Weaver, "Atonement for the Nonconstantinian Church," *Modern Theology* 6 (July 1990) 307–23.
[3] *NH Hyp. Arch.* 93:22–27, 31.

was discarded for more individualistic theories based on sin and guilt.[4] Once the gospel had been the proclamation of release of those who were formerly deluded and enslaved by the Domination System and its driving spirit, Satan. Now Christ's death came to be seen solely as a personal transaction between the believer and God. A person's soul was now to be judged by its degree of conformity to church moral law and obedience to religious and civil authority. That is, one was evaluated by the degree to which one submitted to socialization into the dominant power system. The sin-forgiveness model of theology no longer portrayed a cosmic-historical-political-psychic conflict between Christ and the Powers on earth, but rather the struggle between the individual and the Devil, with the Devil representing (Blake saw it so clearly!) *rebellion against church and state* and all their laws, civil, criminal, and moral, regardless of how unjust, inhumane, degrading or oppressive they might be. *What the early Christians would have called "kneeling to Caesar" or "complicity with Satan" now became the very essence of faithfulness.* The God of triumphal Christian orthodoxy came to be depicted as wrathfully desiring to kill sinners and torture them for all eternity; they are saved only by God's execution of his own Son in the sinner's place. Like early warning radar, the Gnostics could already see the direction the God-concept was evolving: toward a God indistinguishable from a world-monarch, ruthless in his hatred of frailty and disobedience, and the ultimate guarantor of the status quo.

Thinkers like Marcion had anticipated this development in their reading of the Hebrew Scripture, and had tried to counter it by splitting God so as to hold up the shadow side of reality to awareness. The radical dualism of such thinkers must be seen as an attempt to speak simultaneously of the good and evil sides of reality while still maintaining the absolute goodness of God. By carving up the realm of the spirit between a good Father beyond all knowing and a just, evil, ignorant, or arrogant Demiurge, they were able, at the terrible cost of splitting reality and themselves, to assign a place to the elements of darkness in the socio-spiritual sphere that were slowly sinking out of sight into the orthodox unconscious. But the Gnostics had also abandoned the Christus Victor stance for a salvation of escape, and were impotent to offer a viable · alternative.

Few Christians have risen to Marcion's challenge to critique the image of God thoroughly in the light of the cross. Christians need not

---

[4] Weaver, "Atonement." Matthew Fox has expanded on the consequences of this shift in his *Original Blessing* (Santa Fe: Bear and Co., 1983), a book full of urgently valid insights despite its lack of a radical view of evil or of the role of the Powers.

embrace the simplistic solution of Marcion, but can they afford to continue depicting God as the apex of the pyramid of power and the ultimate enforcer of the laws of tyrants? Who *really* is the God worshiped in the chapels of a Marcos, or of a Somoza, or on Park Avenue?

Those who eke out survival at the base of that pyramid of power recognize immediately the meaning of the Gnostic statement, ". . .[T]he soul is food for the authorities and powers, without which they cannot live."[5] The myth depicts this "eating" as happening *after* death, but the pathos with which it is described indicates that the eating is already going on. Incredibly, the victims are unaware that they are being devoured. Therefore it must be made known to them by revelation. According to the Archontics, for example, Seth was caught up to heaven and ". . .had knowledge of the unnamed power, the good God who is above, and served him and gave many revelations discrediting the maker of the world and the authorities and powers."[6] My contention is that this is an authentic revelation of the actual spirituality of the massive political and social institutions that bestrode the Roman world. The Empire's peace and prosperity, in the face of internal decay and external threat, required the sacrifice of human beings to the system. They were "food for the authorities and powers."

A Manichaean psalm plaintively depicts this sense of loss of self in the face of overwhelming Powers:

> Since I have been bound to the flesh
> I have forgotten my divinity. . .
> I was forced to drink the cup of madness,
> I was forced to turn my hand against myself. . .
> The Powers and Principalities
> Approached and armed themselves against me. . .
> Be an enchanter of Light
> and lay a spell on them till I pass them.[7]

The Gnostics viewed the created world, according to Jonas, as "a power system directed at the enslavement of this transmundane self," and everything from the grand cosmic design down to humanity's psychological constitution serves its fearful purpose. The chief means of that enslavement is ". . .'ignorance' actively inflicted and maintained, i.e., the

---

5 Epiphanius, *Panarion* XL.2.7; Foerster's translation, *Gnosis* 1. 297.
6 Ibid, XL.7.2–3; in Foerster, *Gnosis*, 1. 298.
7 *A Manichaean Hymn*, Allberry 116–117; in Robert Haardt, *Gnosis* (Leiden: E. J. Brill, 1971) 310.

alienation of the self from itself as its pervading natural condition."[8] This goes well beyond propaganda, which is a willful manipulation of the truth, to a societal mystification that is ubiquitous, like the noxious ozone that now permeates our air. "In those the counterfeit spirit has become powerful and led them astray," as one text describes it. This "counterfeit spirit" has not only created our bodies, say the Gnostics, but our very souls themselves. The spiritual organ by which we relate to the world has become an encasement or "terrestrial envelopment" of the higher self or pneuma, blocking its access to the truth. The soul is thus the exponent of the alienated world within us, the internalization of the estranged quality of worldly life. Hence "the world is *in* the soul."[9] The rulers have ". . .powers which are in their powers, that is the souls."[10] From this privileged vantage point in human awareness, the soul operates, as it were, as an advocate for the Archons.

The Gnostics, consequently, were among the first "masters of suspicion." Gnostic psychology taught a profound distrust of one's own inwardness. If the alienating world has *produced* the soul, then the soul is not merely, as in Christian theology, tainted, but inauthentic to the very core. We are, in our creation, primordially false. Contempt for the cosmos thus includes contempt for the very soul itself. "Thus inner-worldly experience is essentially a state of being *possessed* by the world, in the literal, i.e., demonological, sense of the term."[11]

Today this state of being possessed is everywhere apparent. The socio-spiritual forces that power the human social world regard education not as self-formation or social transformation but as personnel-production; religion not as the quest for transcendence but as a means for social control; morality not as the free exercise of a sensitive conscience but as obedience to laws that uphold the powerful. "In these the counterfeit spirit has become powerful and led them astray, and it weighs down the soul and draws it to works of wickedness and casts a sleep upon it" (*NH Apocryphon of John* 26:36–27:11). The Counterfeit Spirit creates, by a crude mimetic artistry, counterfeit spirits to service the Domination System.

Unfortunately, the Gnostics themselves seem to have been either unaware of the social sources of their malaise or unwilling to mention them; Rudolph comments on ". . .the virtual absence of contemporary

---

8   Jonas, "Delimitation of the Gnostic Phenomenon" 98.
9   Jonas, *GR* 269.
10   *Pistis Sophia* I.27; Mead, p. 29.
11   Jonas, *GR* 282, italics his.

historical allusions or even of criticism of the Roman imperium. . ." in Gnostic works.[12] Their social protest seems to have been transmuted almost entirely into the afterlife. This, plus the well-known reluctance of Gnostics to suffer martyrdom, led them to adopt a policy of dissembling before earthly authorities. Instead of making the invisible Powers visible and engaging them in spiritual combat, the visible Gnostic was made invisible. The Powers could no longer see them.[13] They practiced an "intellectual reservation" when required to burn incense before the effigy of the emperor, and went along, convinced that God alone could read the heart. They attacked as "foolish" those Christians who "confessed" Christ and paid with martyrdom: "It is slavery that we shall die with Christ."[14]

The Gnostics justified this behavior in their myths; both Sophia and Christ had practiced deception on the Archons of the seven planets and their emperor, the Demiurge.[15] The Gnostic is promised safe-conduct past the Archons via passwords: "I have taught you what to say before the archons."[16] This echoes Luke 12:11–12—"And when they bring you

---

[12] Rudolph, *Gnosis* 265. He continues, however, "Still, one does find a whole series of allusions, direct as well as indirect, to socio-critical views of the gnostics, which differed considerably from those of their own environment." The entire vocabulary of the heavenly powers had its "origin in the political nomenclature of antiquity," not only in references to *archontes* and *exousiai* but even allusions to the commanders of the seven planets through which the soul must pass as "tax gatherers" or "toll collectors" (*Acts of Thomas* 167 [NT Apoc 2. 529]; NH Apoc. Paul 20:16; 22:20; 33:5–20; *Left Ginza* III, 512, 10 and 532, 30–534, 13; *The Book of John* II, 180, 22–181, 8— Mandaean texts in Haardt, *Gnosis* 386–89), or even "administrators" (*Poimandres*, *Corp. Herm.* I.9.14.16; in Foerster, *Gnosis* 1. 330).

[13] Irenaeus, *Against Heresy* I.13.6.

[14] *NH Treat. Seth* 49:26–27; see also *NH Testim. Truth* 31:22–34:26; and the *Two Books of Jeu* (NT Apoc. 1. 261): "Blessed is he who has crucified the world, and has not allowed the world to crucify him." Basilides, according to Clement of Alexandria, went so far as to argue that martyrdom was God's punishment for undetected sins; hence martyrs suffer knowing they deserve it though others do not. Or, perhaps they wanted to sin but simply had no occasion to do so. "Even if he has done nothing bad, I will call him bad because he wanted to sin. For I will say anything rather than call Providence bad" (*Stromateis*. IV.12 section 82.2). It is difficult to suppress doubts concerning the accuracy of Clement's report.

Not all Gnostics condemned martyrdom; see Elaine Pagels, "Gnostic and Orthodox Views of Christ's Passion: Paradigms for the Christian's Response to Persecution?" RG 1. 262–88.

[15] *NH Zost.* 10:15–17; *NH Treat. Seth* 51:20–52:10; 55:10–57:6; *NH Trim. Prot.* 40:8– 41:1; *NH Paraph. Shem* 19:13–20:1; and in Manichaeism generally, the idea that God used the Primordial Man as a baited hook for catching the powers of darkness.

[16] *NH Ap. Jas.* 8:35–36.

before the synagogues and the principalities (*archas*) and the powers (*exousias*), do not be anxious how or what you are to answer or what you are to say; for the Holy Spirit will teach you in that very hour what you ought to say." But these Gnostic Archons are no longer rulers of the synagogues, chief priests, and Roman magistrates and governors; they are heavenly beings cut off from their earthly manifestations. The Gnostics were able to discern the devouring spirits of the institutions they encountered, institutions which most of their contemporaries were all too eager to prostrate themselves before in self-stupefying worship. But their fear of the Powers, indicated by their abhorrence of martyrdom, and their lack of a hermeneutical key, prevented their identifying the real politico-spiritual origin of their distress.

Thus *NH* 1 *Apocalypse of James* recognizes that Jerusalem ". . .is a dwelling place of a great number of archons" and ". . .always gives the cup of bitterness to the sons of light" (25:16–19). But rather than engaging these Powers, as Jesus did by going to Jerusalem, and as James himself actually did by staying and being martyred there, the "James" of this apocalypse is advised to "leave Jerusalem" (25:15), that is, to distance himself from the world and ascend mystically to the higher realm.

In one area the Gnostics made no attempt to mystify the target of their withering social criticism, however, and that was religion. Since they emphasized a personal experience of awakening or rebirth or resurrection as an event that takes place in *this* life, they saw no need for a priestly hierarchy to mediate grace. And they certainly needed no one to pontificate about true knowledge when they could be privy to direct revelations themselves. Some of them dispensed with ordained priests altogether, and rotated leadership, even allowing visitors or novices to direct their hymns and prayers, a practice that vexed Tertullian no end.[17]

Others were not hostile to ecclesiastical offices; some even held high positions in Christian churches. The less spiritual "psychics" still needed leaders to instruct them. What the Gnostics objected to was the claim made by the orthodox that apart from bishops, presbyters and deacons, ". . .one can no longer speak of a church" (Ignatius, *To the Trall.* 3.1), and that "If someone does something without the bishop he does it in vain" (Syriac *Didascalia Apostolorum* 9). The Gnostic could see in such remarks, says Klaus Koschorke, evidence of the greatest deception of the archons. Such a view, they held, ties salvation to something purely external, and utterly abandons the pneumatic-charismatic church order championed

---

[17] Tertullian, *Prescription against Heretics* 41.

by Paul. They ascribed to archontic delusion the futile claim of church leaders that they alone could provide access to God, or that they alone were in possession of the mystery of truth, or that the sacrament was itself sufficient for salvation without the experience of awakening through gnosis.[18] In fact, the Gnostics went so far as to identify the bishops and priests of the Christian church with the "rulers and powers" who govern earth in the name of the Demiurge.[19] Likewise, they continued the prophetic critique of all religious ritual, pagan and Christian alike, even putting their finger squarely on a problem still unresolved to this day: how Christians can continue, after baptism, to ". . .hasten toward the principalities and the authorities" and ". . .fall into their clutches because of the ignorance that is in them."[20]

---

[18] Klaus Koschorke, "Gnostic Instructions on the Organization of the Congregation," *RG* 2. 762–69.

[19] The Valentinians, according to Pagels, *The Gnostic Gospels* (New York: Random House, 1979), 38, citing Irenaeus, *Against Heresy* I.7.4. See also her "'The Demiurge and His Archons'—A Gnostic View of the Bishop and Presbyters?" *HTR* 69 (1976) 301–24.

[20] *NH Test. Truth* 32:4–8. The context refers to martyrdom, but characterizes the Gnostic attitude toward Christians generally.

4

SALVATION FROM THE POWERS

For the Gnostic, liberation from the Rulers of this world involves a revealer or a revelation capable of waking up the sleepers and unmasking the system that cast its spell over them.

1. *Waking up, sobering up.* Given the Gnostics' socio-spiritual analysis, the chief problem of humanity cannot be personal sin, because sin usually presupposes a fixed moral code, and the Gnostics perceived that moral codes are highly relative and a consequence of the process of socialization. Socialization was itself precisely the problem, they saw, for what people are socialized into is a cultural trance. The task of Gnostic salvation is not then to repent of disobedience to some externally imposed code, even the church's, insofar as it shares the cultural trance— but to wake up from the trance itself, to shake off sleep, to sober up from drunkenness. *NH Gospel of Thomas*, though it may not be fully Gnostic, sums up the Gnostic position admirably:

> Jesus said, 'I took my place in the midst of the world, and I appeared to them in flesh. I found all of them intoxicated; I found none of them thirsty. And my soul became afflicted for the sons of men, because they are blind in their hearts and do not have sight. . .. For the moment they are intoxicated. When they shake off their wine, then they will repent' (28).

I believe that recovery of this insight is essential for Christianity as well if it is to take the Powers seriously. The notion of awakening is represented in Scripture, though underutilized: "Awake, O sleeper, and arise from the dead, and Christ shall give you light" (Eph 5:14).[1] What may be the earliest New Testament writing already exhibits a connection between sleep and drunkenness: "For you are all sons of light and sons of the day; we are not of the night or of darkness. So then let us not sleep, as others do, but let us keep awake and be sober. For those who get drunk are drunk at night" (1 Thess 5:5–7). Paul already had transcended a moralistic notion of sin and spoke of it rather as a Power that over-whelms us and takes us hostage. For that reason he seems to have avoided references to repentance and forgiveness, preferring images that stressed our inability to break free of sin by ourselves through an act of will. Thus he spoke of ransom from slavery, justification by the law court, redemption through the sacrifice of another, awakening from a trance-induced sleep, or sobering up from drunkenness, making clear in a variety of images that we are sold in sin and cannot be released apart from the action of a Deliverer.

Paul differed from the Gnostics, however, in his more dialectical attitude toward socialization, seeing the process of enculturation and education as, on the one hand, absolutely essential for inculcating values, transmitting tradition, and checking human greed and violence, and on the other as a bondage that stifles the spirit. Hence he could speak of the Law (a category that for him encompassed religion, culture, mores, tradi-tion, and socialization generally) as both "holy and just and good" (Rom 7:12) and as "that which held us captive" (Rom 7:6). Humanity is always just one generation from reverting to barbarity; we need law as a means to restrain sin. But the very law that preserves our lives from anarchy and reveals God's judgment on sin "kills" (2 Cor 3:6) by imposing con-formity to laws which have themselves been subverted by sin and serve the cause of domination.

For us today, sleep, drunkenness and thralldom are especially apt as metaphors. Ours is a society of addicts. Tens of millions of lives have been taken hostage by powers beyond people's ability to moderate or control: drugs, alcohol, cigarettes, money, food, sex, work, religion, the state. Our best brains in government, the military, and even the church,

---

[1]   See George MacRae, "Sleep and Awakening in Gnostic Texts," *OG* 505. See also *Corp. Herm.* 1.27—"You people, earthborn men, who have given yourselves up to drunkenness and sleep and to ignorance of God, sober up, stop being drunk, bewitched by unreasoning sleep;" and *NH Apoc. Adam* 65:23–25. *NH Gos. Thom.* 28 contrasts drunkenness, not with sobriety, but with not thirsting for the drink that one drinks from Jesus' mouth, i.e., his wisdom (*Gos. Thom.* 13). See Stevan L. Davies, *The Gospel of Thomas and Christian Wisdom* (New York: Seabury Press, 1983) 96.

blessed the nuclear arms race with somnambulistic accord. We watch, spellbound, like insects paralyzed by the sting of a wasp, as our streets fill with the homeless and with drug dealers, unable to muster the moral outrage to change the economic and political system that fuels such tragedy. All too many clergy, terrified for their jobs, dare not criticize the Powers that feed them (or rather, feed upon them), becoming all the more punctilious in their orthodoxy, as if to cover the act of apostasy with zeal against heresy. We are mesmerized, held in thrall by the power of a system that rewards its advocates and destroys its opponents. And this is not just true of our system; it is true to varying degrees of every system on earth. To become sober, then, one needs to be awakened to the cause of one's stupor. The Powers must be unmasked by an act of revelation.

2. *Unmasking the Powers*. The *NH Gos. Phil.* urges,

> Let each of us dig down after the root of evil that is within us, and let us pluck it out of our hearts from the root. It will be plucked out if we recognize it. But if we are ignorant of it, it takes root in us and produces its fruit in our heart. It masters us. We are its slaves. It takes us captive, to make us do what we do not want; and what we do want we do not do. It is powerful because we have not recognized it. While it exists it is active. (83:18–30, modified)

This is not "esoteric" knowledge divulged grudgingly and at great expense in an occult sect. It is recognition of the obvious truth that no one sees. It is a secret hidden in plain sight, in front of everyone's nose. The "mystery" is that people are blind to their thralldom to a ubiquitous and pernicious system that flourishes by robbing people of the authenticity of their true selves and relationships. It is, above all, the revelation of one's own complicity and even joyful collaboration in the suppression of one's most essential human qualities.

It is this collusion in our own oppression that caused the Gnostics such horror, and led them to depreciate everything within them that could stoop to such self-debasement: the conscious mind, reason, one's dominant self-understanding (the socialized "I"), the sexual organs, the body itself, eros, even the soul. Only the higher self, the spiritual spark from on high, retains its integrity, and one knows this by virtue of one's very capacity to recognize one's bondage. This then forms the core of the Gnostic's certainty: everyone capable of recognizing their thralldom to the Domination System shows, by that very capacity, that they are "elect." One's *gnosis* (insight) is itself a gift of grace that must be fought hard to retain against the ongoing assaults of the socio-spiritual order.

This insight saves one, because the very awakening to the fact that the world is sunk under the tyranny of an alienating and alienated order is itself the first act of liberation. Unmasking is already a down payment on deliverance.

Later Gnostics became obsessed with passwords that would guarantee safe passage after death through the seven planetary spheres and their greedy Archons ("Toll Collectors"), but this is a debasement of the primary religious experience: the rediscovery of one's own authentic selfhood, the rescue of the lost "pearl" guarded by the dragon in the far country, the retrieval of the gold in the mud.

This point cannot be overstressed: the experiential bedrock on which the whole of Gnostic religion rests is the sense of release that has *already occurred* through enlightenment as to the real nature of the world and one's part in it. This is an existential, not a propositional, revelation. The "already" is the present assurance of the reality of the "not yet." One is freed from the alienated world through an act of transcendence ("resurrection"), and this has already taken place through gnosis (revelatory insight). Hence the Gnostic cannot doubt the resurrection, for it is precisely the experience of awakening to reality. Resurrection is not a future, promised hope but a present, certain fact. For ". . .it is always the disclosure of those who have risen. . .. Do not think the resurrection is an illusion. It is no illusion, but it is truth! Indeed, it is more fitting to say that the world is an illusion, rather than the resurrection. . .. Already you have the resurrection."[2]

The need for a narrative to explain how the soul became estranged from its Source also accounts for the wild proliferation of stories of the birth of the world and the gods; these myths explained *how* the Domination System of the Archons came to be. The famous Valentinian definition of Gnosticism, "It is *gnosis* of who we were, what we have become; whence we were; into what we have been cast; whither we hasten; whence we are redeemed; what birth is, and what rebirth,"[3] becomes transparent on this reading. The apparent answer to "whence," that one comes from the earth, from one's parents, from the act of coitus, cannot be correct on their terms. For the divine spark awakened by revelation, which alone was able to shatter the crust of socialization, cannot itself have been the product of that depraved socialization or the spiritual

---

[2]   *NH Treat. Res.* 48:4–49:26. Barbara Aland makes a similar point when she finds at the core of the Gnostic religious experience a sense of boundless joy and infinite freedom resulting from redemption ("Gnosis und Christentum," *RG* 1. 319–53).

[3]   *Excerpts from Theodotus* 78.2.

forces that maintain it. The answer must be, according to them: this body is from earth, but the essential self, hitherto unknown, is from a spiritual world beyond this prison in which we dwell. And since the single most powerful impression one gets about this essential or higher self is that it is authentic and knows a truth that the world does not, then the higher spiritual world from which it comes must be one of unsullied goodness and truth. How then did this pearl of perfection from beyond the heavens become impacted in the slime of matter and the system of the Powers? To explain that requires a narrative, and while the details of the story vary from one document to another, the basic pattern remains the same: how the soul became captured in the world, and how it can find its way back to its divine origin. The *NH Gos. Thom.* 56 sums it up concisely: "Whoever has come to understand the world has found (only) a corpse, and whoever has found a corpse is superior to the world."

Christians today can scarcely give total assent to any view that attempts to ascribe all personal evil to social causes. We know too much about the inner shadow to locate all evil outside the self—though that view continues to seduce distinguished proponents. The Gnostics could not tolerate the ambiguity of an evil that is intrinsic to the person *as well as* a consequence of the socialization of the Powers. But to a church that moralizes sin and blames the victims of the Powers, Gnosticism's one-sided critique has a refreshing alienness that can serve to jar Christianity out of its cultural trance and arm it to confront the Principalities and Powers.

Likewise, the Gnostic instinct was correct in locating God beyond the realm of deceit and thralldom, beyond the world system, beyond the realm of the Powers. It is quite true that to be liberated from the Domination System we must be liberated by something outside the Domination System. The error lay in locating that transcendence in a hyper-heaven. God is clearly not a part of the Domination System. God transcends it, however, not by vacating the created world and superannuating to a space beyond space, but by pressing into the present world system with a new and different system, God's domination-free order: the Reign of God. From a Christian perspective, God transcends the world system the way a person fully awake transcends the delusory reality of a sleepwalker.

5 | ETHICS

No area of Gnostic religion should be more revealing of its understanding of the Powers than its ethics, yet it is precisely here that our sources leave us in greatest confusion. The problem is compounded by the sheer variety of Gnostic opinions and behaviors. Nothing is gained by treating Gnosticism as a single phenomenon with a uniform meaning. It was once popular to infer from their antipathy to life in the flesh that they became either ascetics fighting bodily passions, or libertines indulging themselves in every form of licentiousness, since the body is irrelevant to the spirit's salvation. It is now clear that such a view is an oversimplification. Gnostics were probably indistinguishable in most cases from orthodox Christians, with some celibate and ascetic, others married and continent, others married and producing families, and a tiny fraction experimenting sexually and communally.

The Church Fathers were particularly obsessed with Gnostic sexual practices. No doubt some Gnostics engaged in sexual libertinism. Already some in the Corinthian church in the time of Paul were justifying prostitution (1 Cor 6:12–20) and other forms of sexual license (10:8); one member was actually sleeping with his step-mother (5:1). But such practices were probably never widespread in any period. The early apologists for the church could all too easily use sensational reports of such practices to tar all other Gnostics (even ascetic Gnostics) and thus discredit the whole movement. We must remember that the early Christians themselves had been falsely accused of many of these things by the pagans, just as medieval Christians were in turn to malign Jews for murdering and eating Christian babies. Justin and Irenaeus, after giving out as fact the rumors they have heard about the Gnostic revelries, admit that they do not really know for sure ". . .if they practice those fabled disreputable activities."[1] Epiphanius, whose voyeuristic accounts of sexual extravagances among the Gnostics so alarmed his bishop that he excommunicated some ninety people, admits that he did not flee the enticements offered him by these heretics when he saw these deeds done, but only when he *read* about them. Michael A. Williams surveys all the evidence for Gnostic libertinism and concludes that little of it is credible.[2]

When the Gnostics are able to speak for themselves, as they are now better able to do thanks to the Nag Hammadi and other finds, they do not encourage licentiousness.[3] There is not a single clear statement in the entire Nag Hammadi library that justifies sexual promiscuity, and innumerable ones that condemn, not only promiscuity, but sexuality itself.[4] It

---

[1] Justin, *Apology* I.26.7; Irenaeus, *Against Heresy* I.25.5; see R. M. Grant, "Charges of 'Immorality' against Various Religious Groups in Antiquity," *SGHR* 161–70; Stephen Benko, "Pagan Criticism of Christianity during the First Two Centuries," *ANRW* II.23.2 (ed. H. Temporina and W. Haase; New York and Berlin: Walter de Gruyter, 1980) 1055–1118; and Henry Chadwick, "The Domestication of Gnosis," *RG* 1. 5–11. *Pistis Sophia* regards homosexuality and the making of a lentil porridge from "male seed and the female monthly blood" and eating it sacramentally, as "more heinous than all sins and iniquities" (147; Mead, pp. 321–22). From the way the practice is described, it is not apparently commonplace, but rather a rare occurrence—indeed, the most horrible thing of which the author had ever heard, and possibly by hearsay (Mead, p. xxxiv). And the *Two Books of Jeu* 43 roundly condemns those who behave thus; "their God is wicked" (MacDermot, p. 129).

[2] M. A. Williams, "Freedom by Abuse or Freedom by Non-use = Gnostic Ethics?" paper given at the Nag Hammadi and Gnosticism section, annual meeting of the Society of Biblical Literature, San Francisco, 1992. I also benefitted from the paper by Karen L. King, "Neither Libertine Nor Ascetic: A New Look at Gnostic Ethics," given at the same session.

[3] For example, Irenaeus reports of Valentinians that they believed that the Father and the Son both had intercourse with the Holy Spirit/First Mother (*Against Heresies* I.30.1–2). But there is no trace of this incest in the Valentinian texts from Nag Hammadi (Anne Marie McGuire, *Valentinus and the Gnostike Heiresis*, PhD dissertation, Yale University [Ann Arbor: University Microfilms, 1985] 108–109).

[4] *NH Testim. Truth* 57:6–60:4 may refer to libertinism, but it is conjectural at best because of lacunae in the text. G. A. G. Stroumsa notes that in the history of religions, ascetic behavior and sexually-centered mythology often go together, and speculates that the Church Fathers misinterpreted the mythology as a reflection of actual practice (*Another Seed: Studies in Gnostic Mythology* [Leiden: E. J. Brill, 1984] 173). It seems likely, however, that some of the Gnostics took their mythology literally as well. See also Richard Smith, "Sex Education in Gnostic Schools," *IFG* 345–60.

The strong ascetic tendencies in Gnosticism were in part a trend of the period; orthodox Christianity and pagan philosophy also embraced asceticism in a new way. See Vincent L. Wimbush, *Renunciation as Social Engineering* (Occasional Papers 8; Claremont: Institute for Antiquity and Christianity, 1986); and Peter Brown, *The Body*

is axiomatic in religious polemic that people tend to evaluate their own religious position in terms of its best exemplars, and the religions they wish to attack by their worst. It is simply not true that what happened in the body was a matter of indifference to most Gnostics. "The Gnostic must strive to realize the same separation in this life that he hopes to attain when he is finally freed from the bondage of cosmic reality."[5]

Yet the sheer frequency of mythological depictions of the union of the opposites was bound to be taken literally at times and acted out, both rebelliously (in defiance of the moral code of one's upbringing) and ritually (in sincere imitation of the divine process). Thus pseudo-Macarius warns the Messalians (a fourth century sect of Syria and Asia Minor accused of wild promiscuity) against taking the image of the soul as a wife too literally.[6] If seduction and clergy sexual abuse and even orgies crop up in Christian churches today, despite stern condemnations of such behavior, they probably took place among the Gnostics as well. But there is a great gulf between occasional aberrations and esteemed teachings. The fact is that there is only the slimmest of evidence that any Gnostics advocated licentious behavior. They were not so much libertine as libertarian.[7]

What the Church Fathers were reacting to may have simply been the fact that Gnostics apparently rejected any attempt to impose a set of rules for sexual behavior, one way or another. Addiction to any earthly thing is denounced, whether to wealth, or sexual intercourse, or food, or clothing, or ostentation, or envy of others—a position common to all high religions.[8] But what we find missing in Gnostic sources is the pre-occupation with behavior that provoked the lists of moral advice (the *Haustafeln*) that characterized the later New Testament epistles, or the day-to-day conflict over ethical norms and actions that animate Paul's Corinthian correspondence. Apparently the Gnostics believed that individuals were capable of choosing for themselves what is right, a teaching they could, if they wished, trace to Jesus himself (Luke 12:57). That some

---

and Society: Men, Women, and Sexual Renunciation in Early Christianity (New York: Columbia University, 1988).

[5] Perkins, *The Gnostic Dialogue* 189. So also M. R. Desjardins, *Sin in Valentinianism* (SBLDS 108; Atlanta: Scholars Press, 1987).

[6] Giovani Filoramo, *A History of Gnosticism* (Oxford: Basil Blackwell, 1991) 185.

[7] Stephan A. Hoeller, *The Gnostic Jung* (Wheaton: Theosophical Publishing House, 1989) 41.

[8] *NH Auth. Teach.* 30:26–32:3. On the subject generally, see Rudolph, *Gnosis* 262–72.

proved incapable of such supreme trust merely indicates the costliness of this path, not its error.

A sharp contradiction exists within our sources regarding the place of women. Some texts unmask the illegitimacy of male domination, feature feminine redeemer figures, and caricature the male Demiurge and his archons as bumbling fools. Gnostic women clearly did exercise more leadership functions than did women in the repatriarchalized Christian Church; Gnosticism may in fact have been a haven for women squeezed out of leadership roles in orthodox churches. Some of the surviving Gnostic documents and apocryphal Gospels may even have been written by women.

The NH *Hypostasis of the Archons* may be one such text;[9] it identifies patriarchy, male lust, and the Domination System as a single life-crushing deceit imposed on the world by the (male) Archons. In 89:17–30 the Archons who created the world lust after the pneumatic or heavenly Eve. They pursue her, saying, "Come, let us sow our seed in her." But "she laughed at them for their witlessness and their blindness; and in their clutches, she became a tree, and left before them her shadowy reflection resembling herself"—an allusion to the tendency of sexually abused women to dissociate from their bodies?—"and they defiled it foully." These Archons are equated with Yahweh, and are portrayed as hating anything higher than themselves and wanting to drag down, sully, and contaminate the spiritual by inseminating it with their own defiling lusts. This hatred of the divine is portrayed as the desire to dominate, rape, and domesticate a female. Such an account certainly appears to have been written from a woman's perspective.[10]

---

[9] Birger A. Pearson argues that the second main part of the *Hyp. Arch.* may be based on an "Apocalypse of Norea" written by a woman, and other writings ascribed to Norea may have been written by female Sethian Gnostics as well ("Revisiting Norea," *IFG* 272–73). Likewise, Madeleine Scopello suggests that *NH Exeg. Soul* was possibly written by a woman ("Jewish and Greek Heroines in the Nag Hammadi Library," *IFG* 90), and Stevan L. Davies believes that some of the apocryphal Acts were authored by women (*The Revolt of the Widows: The Social World of the Apocryphal Acts* [Carbondale: Southern Illinois University Press, 1980]).

[10] See Anne McGuire, "Virginity and Subversion: Norea Against the Powers in the *Hypostasis of the Archons*," *IFG* 239–58. Rose Horman Arthur, however, sees *Hyp. Arch.* as a Christianization and repatriarchalization of the mythology reflected in *Orig. World*, resulting in the suppression of the feminine character of the world soul, the blaming of Sophia for all the evil in the world, and the depiction of her motivation as mimetic envy and of her salvation as mediated through a male aeon, Christ/Holy Spirit (*The Wisdom Goddess* [Lanham: University Press of America, 1984] 5–7, 93–156).

The more common Gnostic view, however, is that the female represents materiality and sexuality; both women and men are called to reject femininity and become male. Another view is that both become genderless in the spiritual realm above—which, however, continues to be modeled along patriarchal lines.[11]

Simonian Gnosticism, as described by Irenaeus, lifts up another aspect of Gnosticism's withering social critique: the attack on legalism. The Old Testament laws, according to the traditions associated with Simon Magus, were inspired by fallen angels. The works required by its laws are not ". . .just by nature, but by convention, as the angels who made the world ordained, in order to enslave humanity by such precepts."[12] Such legal constraints are the very means by which the individual is integrated into and made subservient to the demiurgal scheme.[13] This view of the law is, like the Gnostic view of the Powers, non-dialectical; such a position was bound to lead, at times at least, to libertinism, since it failed to recognize, as Paul did so clearly, that law is both indispensable and unendurable.

A more considered statement (and remember, the above digest of Simon's views was penned by a hostile critic) is found in the *NH Gos.*

---

[11] Karen L. King, "Ridicule and Rape, Rule and Rebellion: Images of Gender in *The Hypostasis of the Archons*," in *Gnosticism and the Early Christian World: Festschrift for James M. Robinson* (ed. James A. Sanders and Charles Hedrick; Sonoma: Polebridge Press, 1990) 1–35; also her "Eve, Mary and Sophia: Images of the Feminine in the Non-Canonical Gospels," not yet published. Norea is significant in the *Hyp. Arch.* because she represents a female deity able to depotentiate the Archons through *gnosis*, rather than simply fleeing them to the world above (Ingvild Saelid Gilhus, *The Nature of the Archons* [SOR 12; Wiesbaden: Otto Harrassowitz, 1985] 113). This text gives us a faint glimpse of how Gnosticism might have developed had it chosen to confront, rather than to elude, the Powers. See also Anne McGuire, "Virginity and Subversion" 257: "The unmasking of illegitimate male domination by female figures of spiritual power proved to be a powerful vehicle for the expression of the gnostic revolt against the powers."

Jung considers the story of the "fall" of Sophia to be a psychological depiction, in the form of cosmically projected myth, of the "separation of the feminine anima from a masculine and spiritually oriented consciousness that strives for the final and absolute victory of the spirit over the world of the senses, as was the case in the pagan philosophies of that epoch no less than in Gnosticism" (*Alchemical Studies,* Collected Works 13 [1967] 335). If he is right, the myth of Sophia's fall reflects a compensatory reaction to the hypertrophy of the intellect in the psyches of *males,* and is not an instance of a female "heroine" in myth. (She is, after all, scapegoated for all the evil in the world!)

[12] Irenaeus, *Against Heresy* I.23.3; in Foerster, *Gnosis* 1. 31.

[13] Jonas, *GR* 272.

Phil.: "In this world there is good and evil. Its good things are not good, and its evil things not evil. But there is evil after this world which is truly evil" (66:10–14). This saying recognizes that what society dubs "good" and "evil" are not necessarily so, while avoiding complete relativism by positing real evil as defined by the true God.

The Gnostics avowed, with a one-sidedness that is breathtaking, that all law—civil, religious, moral—is the outworking of the spirituality of the Domination System. Laws are required by the System in order to compel people to surrender their freedom, lands, wealth, even lives, to the maintenance of an order that benefits but a few while exploiting the many. Such a system, the Gnostics urged, was fundamentally non-reformable. But neither did they look for a new heaven and a new earth from God, where human needs *are* met, as does the New Testament. Rather, the entire created world must be dissolved. With that dissolution, however, the socio-political value of their critique dissolved as well, since it was dissociated from its referent in the external world.

Some Gnostics allegedly argued that one could only prove one's freedom from the Archons by breaking every law of conventional morality. If the charge is true (and that is debatable), the Archons would still be determining behavior, only now they do so by defining the rules that one must *violate*. This stance is simply adolescent rebellion elevated to metaphysical status, and it is unlikely that mature Gnostics were taken in by it. And "breaking every law" certainly did not include murder. Apparently sexual mores were all they meant.

The *NH 2 Treatise of the Great Seth* gives a more balanced statement, one that does justice to Paul's most radical assertions about the law: The pneumatic needs no law, legal codes, or prohibitions to guide behavior because such a person unites entirely ". . .with his will which belongs alone to the insight of the Fatherhood, that it (the Fatherhood) may again become perfect."[14] This is the statement of a profound mysticism, worthy of any of the higher religions. It also runs the risk of a towering inflation, since it does not acknowledge the way unredeemed shadow elements in the psyche and in society contaminate our willing.

It is easy to see how someone still caught in the Domination System, still rebellious against authority without having found her or his own inner authority or God's, could mishandle such sovereign moral freedom. But it is the very position taken by John's Gospel ("This is my commandment, that you love one another," John 15:12) and later by the

---

[14] *NH Treat. Seth* 61:30–35; Rudolph's translation, *Gnosis* 118.

former Manichaean Gnostic, Augustine ("Love God and do as you please").[15] What sounds like libertinism to a person still subject to external authority is simply a statement about inner-directed self-control to a person centered in God. The same insight that enables transformation in the mature can lead to catastrophe for the immature. As Paul had already said, "Yet among the mature we do impart wisdom, although it is not a wisdom of this age or of the rulers (*archons*) of this age, who are doomed to pass away" (1 Cor 2:6).

Finally, Gnosticism sought not only to subvert law but the very Scriptures that founded it. One at times encounters brilliant exegesis among the Gnostics.[16] At others we encounter a revisionist re-reading of the text, as if the exegete were seeking not so much to understand it as to fight free of its hold over the psyche. The Gnostic wishes, by means of the tradition, to break away from the tradition, yet in such a way that the tradition itself is liberated from its current religious context. One seeks to overthrow the very strongest of all texts, the Bible, not, as Harold Bloom puts it, by means of a deliberate misreading, but by an inversion of viewpoint. This is clearest in their remarkable re-readings of Genesis 1–3. They sought not to destroy the tradition but to recontextualize it.[17] The text is the same, but the language-world has changed.

NH Trimorphic Protennoia 41:23–29 explicitly articulates this process: "And out of the immersion of the mysteries I spoke, I together with the Archons and Authorities. *For I had gone down below their language* and I spoke my mysteries to my own—a hidden mystery—and the bonds and eternal oblivion were nullified." This excavation of language—this going "down below their language"—displaces the text, makes it mobile, allowing it to be roped and towed to a new haven where its words have new meanings that bespeak the new world to which it has been made captive.

This deliberately revisionist re-reading, whose purpose, says Bloom, is to clear away the precursor so as to open a space for the new, also characterized Christianity's use of the Hebrew Bible, though far less violence was required. Christians merely retrojected the Christ into the Old Testament and reinterpreted the whole of it as an anticipation of

---

[15] Perhaps if we thought in terms of James Fowler's stages of faith, much of this misunderstanding of Gnosticism would disappear (*Stages of Faith* [San Francisco: Harper & Row, 1981]).

[16] Especially in the "Letter of Ptolemaeus to Flora," in Epiphanius, *Panarion* XXXIII.3.1–7, 10.

[17] Harold Bloom, "Lying Against Time: Gnosis, Poetry, Criticism," *RG* 1. 57–72.

Jesus, which in many ways it was (and in many ways it was not). Anything objectionable could simply be disposed of by the open-sesame of allegorization.

But Gnosticism, in its deepest impulse, was neither fulfillment nor reform. It was the revelation of the end of tradition, the end of cult, law, temple, sacrifice, rules, taboos, mores, bodies, souls, the end of the world itself—everything: an apocalypse of metaphysics. Only the spirit would remain, snatched up to the Unknowable God in the unimaginable beyond. Such a metaphysical lust for destruction has never been witnessed on this good earth before or since.

6 | Conclusion

I have attempted in this essay to appreciate the role of the Powers in Gnosticism and to reinterpret them, using as our Rosetta stone the theory that the Powers are not "up there" in the sky but are rather the outer and inner aspects of real entities in this one and only social-physical-spiritual world. Having been misunderstood more than once in my life, I wish to write this so that those who run may read: my appreciation for the Gnostic achievement does not make me a Gnostic. I love this created world, life in the body, sexuality, my wife, my children, and the God I encounter in them all. I look for the redemption of the body, this planet, and the whole of creation, not their dissolution. I agree with the Gnostics that humanity is alienated from both nature and nature's Creator, but I believe that this estrangement is not caused by matter and the body but by idolatry and rebellion. I agree with them that the Powers are real, that the God-image has been corrupted by the human lust for power, that all too few people seem to be aware of their divine origin and the soporific effects of the world; but I do not find it necessary to dismiss the Hebrew Bible, or take flight into solipsism, asceticism, self-absorption, or social irresponsibility. Above all, I cannot stomach the Gnostic hatred of the body and creation. The Gnostic litany of body-loathing and world revulsion sometimes sounds like a case of metaphysical anorexia nervosa, a refusal to be incarnated or to make a home in this world.[1] But, curiously enough, I suspect that many of the neo-Gnostics who are abroad today

---

[1] On the worldview of anorexics, see Marion Woodman, *The Owl Was a Baker's Daughter: Obesity, Anorexia Nervosa and the Repressed Feminine* (Toronto: Inner City Books, 1980).

would agree with me. And the church itself, through monastic asceticism, managed to institutionalize and enfold a large part of the Gnostic impulse, in both its more creative and its worst, most negative forms.

Obviously, anyone who can say, "Do not let your mind have dealings with the body,"[2] is well on the way not only to splitting the body from the spirit but also to spiritualizing the Powers and failing to maintain their connection with the actual power structures of the world. In the Gnostic understanding, the coherence of heaven and earth tears apart. Hatred of this world casts it off from the life of God. Hence the Powers are no longer seen as created, fallen, and needing redemption, but as misbegotten abortions requiring destruction. The elegant ambivalence of the New Testament's view of the Powers finally degenerates, in the hands of the Gnostics, to demonism pure and simple. The Powers are not to be recalled to their divine vocation, but abandoned to the abyss. The Gnostic's journey does not lead from one town to the next in an ongoing encounter with actual social evils, but away from this world through the planets and into the blissful beyond. Rather than engaging the Powers head on, as did the plodding and less imaginative orthodox, the Gnostic gives the Powers the slip, vanishing out of their sight through duplicity and finally out of their world entirely.

But then, how does any of this differ from what many Christians experience as Christian fundamentalism? And are enculturated Christians today any less fearful of martyrdom than the Gnostics were? In short, it has become devilishly hard nowadays to tell a Gnostic from a Christian![3]

I do not see it as my task, however, to issue the usual concluding "refutation of all Gnostic heresies." I have been concerned, rather, to recover, through an act of hermeneutical divination, the understanding

---

[2] *NH Paraph. Shem* 41:5–7, 1st ed.

[3] See Philip J. Lee's *Against the Protestant Gnostics* (New York/Oxford: Oxford University, 1987), which, despite its perfectly valid criticisms of gnosticism within Christianity, still falls in the genre of "Against All Heresies" literature and thus misses the opportunity to learn anything from Gnosticism.

More polemical and problematic is Carl A. Raschke's *The Interruption of Eternity: Modern Gnosticism and the Origins of the New Religious Consciousness* (Chicago: Nelson-Hall, 1980). The author never defines Gnosticism, and consequently is able to tar every idea or thinker he dislikes as "gnostic." He labels "Gnostic" Nietzsche, the German romantics, Jung, Aldous Huxley, Mircea Eliade, Hinduism, Nazism, Zen Buddhism, and the Beat Generation. If Gnosticism is characterized by anything, it is the rejection of the body and valuation only of spirit; but Raschke labels Alan Watts as Gnostic for *attacking* this split between body and spirit. Despite this fundamental conceptual weakness, however, the book is full of useful observations.

of the principalities and powers in Gnosticism. What the Gnostics saw, in a way that all too few of our social engineers and psychotherapists see today, is that it is the world itself—the system of domination in all its permutations—that must be overcome, not our alienation from such a world. And they correctly discerned, as Jonas notes, that a world degraded to a power system can only be overcome through power[4]—in their case, spiritual power. From my perspective, they were right: the solution required spiritual transformation. Where they fell short was in making the connection between spiritual alienation and the domination system itself.

In any case I wish to make this appeal: it is no more Christian (or even basically civil) to call someone pejoratively a "Gnostic" than to speak disparagingly of someone as "a Jew." Gnosticism was a mighty adversary, and it deserves the same respect we tend to accord Judaism or Buddhism or other great world religions.

Likewise, the difficulty in arriving at an agreed-upon definition of Gnosticism even in its ancient form should silence us when we are tempted to brand someone a "Gnostic." Gnosticism is above all a historical reality, containing elements that function together as a totality. The mere presence of one or two of its features in some modern system of thought does not stamp it as Gnostic.[5] Just as restoration of a free market would not make China capitalist, so belief in a higher Self does not make Jung a "Gnostic."[6] Nihilism is not "Gnostic" because it is world-rejecting, nor are libertines "Gnostics" because they practice free sex. Meditators are not "Gnostics" because they seek private illumination, nor are New Agers "Gnostic" because they believe in reincarnation and in creating their own reality and in salvation by knowing the latest esoteric fad. Scriptural exegetes are not "Gnostic" just because they stand Scripture on its head, nor are theologians "Gnostics" because they believe the world would be saved if only everyone agreed with their peculiar form of

---

[4] Jonas, *GR* 329.

[5] Th. P. van Baaren, "Towards a Definition of Gnosticism," in *OG* 174–80.

[6] In *The Gnostic Jung*, Stephan A. Hoeller argues that Jung not only interpreted Gnostic texts, but was himself a Gnostic. But Hoeller's definition of Gnosticism is so loose that it lacks all precision. Missing in Jung are any signs of the denigration of the body, a body/soul dualism, the belief that phenomenal reality is the creation of a Demiurge or some other inferior spiritual being, and all speculation about slipping past the archons in an afterlife. Jung no doubt drew upon Gnostic-like experiences (*The Seven Sermons to the Dead*), but he succeeded in transmuting them, along with his reading of Gnostic and alchemical texts, into a quite new psychological and, at times, metaphysical, system.

gnosis. All of these can be fruitfully *compared* with Gnosticism, but as for an actual identity—of their being "Gnostic"—more would be required than mere similarity; what would be required would be an actual repristination of the total impulse.[7]

In a curious way, Gnosticism can help Christians recover a sense of the uniqueness of their own faith, and to locate it historically in the struggle for world that characterized the first centuries of our era. Classical paganism taught the optimistic belief that salvation consists in unity with the physical world. Gnosticism taught escape from a world imprisoned under the tyranny of evil powers. The New Testament teaches liberation from the tyranny of evil powers in order to recover a lost unity with the created world. This world is not only the sphere of alienated existence, but also the object of God's redemptive love. Therefore we are not to flee the world, but to recall it to its Source.

Much of contemporary Christianity has been so culturally compromised for so long that I cannot conceive of its recovering a fresh sense of its mission apart from a renewed understanding of the Powers. And this is precisely where the Gnostics can help us. We cannot go the full distance in their demonization of the Powers, but a demythologized appreciation of their corruption can go a long way toward curing us of our inveterate optimism regarding the Powers' capacities for good. We cannot accept the idea that the political order is depraved pure and simple, but the Gnostics can help shake us out of our bewitched obsequiousness to the regnant civil religion. And, argues Schuyler Brown, Gnostics can help Christians recover the religious imagination that Western rationalism—biblical studies included—has so egregiously stunted.[8]

In sum, Christian-Gnostic dialogue leads us beyond both the Constantinian compromise of Christianity and the world-rejection of the Gnostics to a new acknowledgment of the reality and venality of the principalities and powers, and arms us with powerful symbolic categories for engaging in the struggle against these Powers for a new and better world.

---

[7] Jonas analyzes nihilism in "Gnosticism and Modern Nihilism," *Social Research* 19 (1952) 430–52, and Gilles Quispel takes a hard look at Jung, Hesse, and Faust (*Gnostic Studies* [Leiden: Nederlands Historisch-Archaeologisch Institute te Istanbul, 1975] 241–58 and 288–307). A team of scholars evaluates *Gnosis und Politik*, ed. Jacob Taubes (RPT 2; München: Wilhelm Fink Verlag, 1984), and Carsten Colpe examines "The Challenge of Gnostic Thought for Philosophy, Alchemy, and Literature" (*RG* 1. 32–56).

[8] Schuyler Brown, "Religious Imagination—Then and Now," *Bible Today* 29 (1991) 237–41.

Bibliography

(For the sake of brevity I have included only those works that are cited in the study or that provide indispensable background.)

Aland, B. "Gnosis und Christentum." *RG* 1. 319–53.

Arthur, R. H. *The Wisdom Goddess.* Lanham: University Press of America, 1984.

Attridge, H. W. and Pagels, E., eds. *The Nag Hammadi Codex I.* 2 vols. NHS 22–23. Leiden: E. J. Brill, 1985.

Avens, R. *The New Gnosis.* Dallas: Spring Publications, 1984.

Baaren, Th. P. van "Towards a Definition of Gnosticism." *OG* 175–80.

Benko, S. "Pagan Criticism of Christianity during the First Two Centuries." *ANRW* II.23.2, ed. H. Temporina and W. Haase. New York and Berlin: Walter de Gruyter, 1980, 1055–1118.

Bianchi, U. "Le Problème des origines du Gnosticisme." *Le Origini dello Gnosticismo.* Ed. Bianchi. Leiden: E. J. Brill, 1967.

Blake, W. "Jerusalem." *The Complete Writings of William Blake.* Rev. ed. Ed. David V. Erdman. Berkeley: University of California, 1982.

Bloom, H. "Lying Against Time: Gnosis, Poetry, Criticism." *RG* 1. 57–72.

Broek, R. van den. "Autogenes and Adamas. The Mythological Structure of the Apocryphon of John." *Gnosis and Gnosticism.* Ed. Martin Krause. NHS 17. Leiden: E. J. Brill, 1981, 16–25.

———— and Vermasseren, M. J., eds. *Studies in Gnosticism and Hellenistic Religions. Festschrift for Gilles Quispel.* Leiden: E. J. Brill, 1981.

Brown, P. *The Body and Society: Men, Women, and Sexual Renunciation in Early Christianity.* New York: Columbia University, 1988.

Brown, S. "Religious Imagination—Then and Now." *Bible Today* 29 (1991) 237–41.

Chadwick, H. "The Domestication of Gnosis." *RG* 1. 5–11.

Colpe, C. "The Challenge of Gnostic Thought for Philosophy, Alchemy, and Literature." *RG* 1. 32–56.

Culianu, I. P. "The Angels of the Nations and the Origins of Gnostic Dualism." *SGHR* 78-91.

Davies, S. L. *The Gospel of Thomas and Christian Wisdom.* New York: Seabury Press, 1983.

—— *The Revolt of the Widows: The Social World of the Apocryphal Acts.* Carbondale: Southern Illinois, 1980.

Desjardins, M. R. *Sin in Valentinianism.* SBLDS 108. Atlanta: Scholars Press, 1987.

Dillon, J. "The Descent of the Soul." *RG* 1. 358-59.

Drijvers, H. J. W. "The Origins of Gnosticism as a Religious and Historical Problem." *NedTTs* 22 (1968) 321–51.

Edwards, M. J. "Gnostics and Valentinians in the Church Fathers." *JTS* 40 (1989) 26–47.

Filoramo, G. *A History of Gnosticism.* Oxford: Basil Blackwell, 1991.

Foerster, W. *Gnosis.* Oxford: Clarendon Press, 1972.

Fossum, J. E. *The Name of God and the Angel of the Lord.* WUNT. Tübingen: J. C. B. Mohr, 1985.

Fowler, J. *Stages of Faith.* San Francisco: Harper & Row, 1981.

Fox, M. *Original Blessing.* Santa Fe: Bear and Co., 1983.

Gilhus, I. S. *The Nature of the Archons.* SOR 12. Wiesbaden: Otto Harrassowitz, 1985.

Good, D. J. *Reconstructing the Tradition of Sophia in Gnostic Literature.* SBLMS 32. Atlanta: Scholars Press, 1987.

Grant, R. M. "Charges of 'Immorality' against Various Religious Groups in Antiquity." *SGHR* 161–70.

—— *Gnosticism: An Anthology.* London: Collins, 1961.

—— *Gnosticism and Early Christianity.* New York: Harper & Row, 1966.

Green, H. A. *The Economic and Social Origins of Gnosticism.* Atlanta: Scholars Press, 1985.

Haardt, R. *Gnosis.* Leiden: E. J. Brill, 1971.

Hennecke, E. and Schneemelcher, W. *New Testament Apocrypha.* 2 vols. Philadelphia: Westminster Press, 1965.

Hoeller, S. *The Gnostic Jung.* Wheaton, IL: Theosophical Publishing House, 1989.

Jonas, H. "Delimitation of the Gnostic Phenomenon—Typology and History." *OG* 90–108.

—— "*Evangelium Veritatis* and the Valentinian Speculation." TU 81. *Studia Patristica* 6 (1962) 96–111.

—— *Gnosis und spätantiker Geist.* FRLANT. Göttingen: Vandenhoeck und Ruprecht. Vol. 1, *Die mythologische Gnosis mit einer Einleitung zur Geschichte und Methodologie der Forschung.* 3d ed. 1964. Vol. 2/1, *Von der Mythologie zur mystischen Philosophie.* 2d ed. 1966.

———— *The Gnostic Religion.* 3d ed. Boston: Beacon Press, 1970.

———— "Gnosticism and Modern Nihilism." *Social Research* 19 (1952) 430–52.

———— *Philosophical Essays.* Englewood Cliffs: Prentice-Hall, 1974.

Jung, C. G. *Aion.* Collected Works 9.2, Bollingen Series 20. Princeton: Princeton University, 1959.

———— *Alchemical Studies.* CW 13. Princeton: Princeton University, 1967.

———— *Civilization in Transition.* CW 10. Princeton: Princeton University, 1964.

———— *The Symbolic Life.* CW 18. Princeton: Princeton University, 1980.

———— *Two Essays on Analytical Psychology.* 2nd ed. CW 7. Princeton: Princeton University, 1966.

King, K. L., ed. *Images of the Feminine in Gnosticism.* Philadelphia: Fortress Press, 1988.

———— "Ridicule and Rape, Rule and Rebellion: Images of Gender in *The Hypostasis of the Archons.*" *Gnosticism and the Early Christian World: Festschrift for J. M. Robinson.* Ed. J. A. Sanders and C. Hedrick. Sonoma: Polebridge Press, 1990, 1–35.

———— "Eve, Mary and Sophia: Images of the Feminine in the Non-Canonical Gospels." Unpublished, courtesy of the author.

Kippenberg, H. "Versuch einer soziologischen Verortung des antiken Gnostizismus." *Numen* 17 (1970) 21–32.

Koschorke, K. "Gnostic Instructions on the Organization of the Congregation." *RG* 2. 762–69.

Layton, B. *The Gnostic Scriptures.* Garden City: Doubleday, 1987.

———— "The Hypostasis of the Archons (Conclusion)," *HTR* 69 (1976) 31–101.

———— *The Rediscovery of Gnosticism.* 2 vols. Leiden: E. J. Brill. Vol. 1: *The School of Valentinus,* 1980; Vol. 2: *Sethian Gnosticism,* 1981.

Lee, P. J. *Against the Protestant Gnostics.* New York and Oxford: Oxford University, 1987.

MacDermot, V., tr. *Pistis Sophia.* Ed. C. Schmidt. NHS 9. Leiden: E. J. Brill, 1978).

———— *The Books of Jeu and the Untitled Text in the Bruce Codex.* Ed. C. Schmidt. NHS 13. Leiden: E. J. Brill, 1978.

MacMullen, R. *Soldier and Civilian in the Later Roman Empire.* Cambridge: Harvard University, 1963.

MacRae, G. "Sleep and Awakening in Gnostic Texts." *OG* 496–507.

McGuire, A. M. *Valentinus and the Gnostike Hairesis.* PhD dissertation, Yale University, 1983.

———— "Virginity and Subversion: Norea Against the Powers in the *Hypostasis of the Archons.*" *IFG* 239–58.

Mead, G. R. S., tr. *Pistis Sophia.* London: J. M. Watkins, (1921) 1963.

Munz, P. "The Problem of 'Die Soziologische Verortung des Antiken Gnostizismus.'" *Numen* 19 (1972) 40–51.

Odajnyk, V. W. *Jung and Politics*. New York: Harper & Row, 1976.

Pagels, E. "Conflicting Versions of Valentinian Eschatology: Irenaeus' Treatise vs. *The Excerpts from Theodotus*." *HTR* 67 (1974) 35–53.

———— "'The Demiurge and His Archons'—A Gnostic View of the Bishop and Presbyters?" *HTR* 69 (1976) 301–24.

———— "Gnostic and Orthodox Views of Christ's Passion: Paradigms for the Christian's Response to Persecution?" *RG* 1. 262-88.

———— *The Gnostic Gospels*. New York: Random House, 1979.

Pearson, B. A. "Revisiting Norea." *IFG* 265–75.

Perkins, P. *The Gnostic Dialogue*. New York: Paulist Press, 1980.

Pétrement, S. *A Separate God*. HarperSanFrancisco, 1990.

Progoff, I. *Jung's Psychology and Its Social Meaning*. New York: Anchor Books, [1953] 1973.

Quispel, G. "The Demiurge in the Apocryphon of John." *Nag Hammadi and Gnosis*. Ed. R. McL. Wilson. NHS 14. Leiden: E. J. Brill, 1978.

———— "Gnosis and Psychology." *RG* 1. 31.

———— *Gnostic Studies*. Leiden: Nederlands Historisch-Archaeologisch Institute te Istanbul, 1975.

Raschke, C. A. *The Interruption of Eternity: Modern Gnosticism and the Origins of the New Religious Right*. Chicago: Nelson-Hall, 1980.

Ricoeur, P. *The Symbolism of Evil*. New York: Harper & Row, 1967.

Robinson, J. M., ed. *The Nag Hammadi Library*. Rev. ed. San Francisco: Harper & Row, 1988.

Rudolph, K. *Gnosis*. San Francisco: Harper and Row, 1983.

———— "Das Problem einer Soziologie and 'sozialen Verortung' der Gnosis." *Kairos* 19/1 (1977) 35–44.

Sanford, J. *The Kingdom Within*. Philadelphia: J. B. Lippincott, 1970.

Schattschneider, H. "Physician-Nurse-Patient Relationships: A Nursing Perspective." Master's Thesis, St. Stephen's Theological College, Edmonton, Alberta, 1988.

Scholem, G. G. *Major Trends in Jewish Mysticism*. New York: Schocken Books, 1965.

Schwager, R. *Must There Be Scapegoats?* San Francisco: Harper & Row, 1987.

Scholten, C. "Gibt es Quellen zur Sozialgeschichte der Valentinianer Roms?" *ZNW* 79 (1988) 244–61.

Scopello, M. "Jewish and Greek Heroines in the Nag Hammadi Library." *IFG* 71–90.

Smith, R. "Sex Education in Gnostic Schools." *IFG* 345–60.

Stroumsa, G. A. G. *Another Seed: Studies in Gnostic Mythology*. Leiden: E. J. Brill, 1984.

Taubes, J. *Gnosis und Politik*. RPT 2. München: Wilhelm Fink Verlag, 1984.

Thomassen, E. "The Structure of the Transcendent World in the Tripartite Tractate (NHC I,5)." *Vig. Chr.* 34 (1980) 358–75.

Vallée, G. *A Study in Anti-Gnostic Polemics.* SCJ/ECJ 1. Waterloo: Wilfred Laurier University, 1981.

Weaver, J. D. "Atonement for the Nonconstantinian Church." *Modern Theology* 6 (1990) 307–23.

Wimbush, V. L., ed. *Renunciation in Early Christianity.* Occasional Papers 8. Claremont: Institute for Antiquity and Christianity, 1986.

Wink, W. *Engaging the Powers. Discernment and Resistance in a World of Domination.* Minneapolis: Fortress Press, 1992.

——— *Naming the Powers. The Language of Power in the New Testament.* Philadelphia: Fortress Press, 1984.

——— *Unmasking the Powers. The Invisible Forces That Determine Human Existence.* Philadelphia: Fortress Press, 1986.

Woodman, M. *The Owl Was a Baker's Daughter: Obesity, Anorexia Nervosa and the Repressed Feminine.* Toronto: Inner City Books, 1980.

Yamauchi, E. M. "Jewish Gnosticism." *SGHR* 467–97.

Index of Names

Index of Texts

Index of Subjects